yourself

training

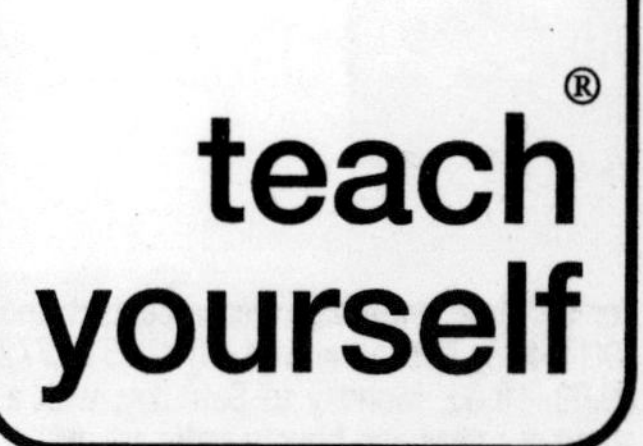

training

bernice walmsley

For over 60 years, more than 40 million people have learnt over 750 subjects the **teach yourself** way, with impressive results.

be where you want to be with **teach yourself**

For UK order enquiries: please contact Bookpoint Ltd, 130 Milton Park, Abingdon, Oxon OX14 4SB. Telephone: +44 (0) 1235 827720. Fax: +44 (0) 1235 400454. Lines are open 09.00–18.00, Monday to Saturday, with a 24-hour message answering service. Details about our titles and how to order are available at www.teachyourself.co.uk

For USA order enquiries: please contact McGraw-Hill Customer Services, PO Box 545, Blacklick, OH 43004-0545, USA. Telephone: 1-800-722-4726. Fax: 1-614-755-5645.

For Canada order enquiries: please contact McGraw-Hill Ryerson Ltd, 300 Water St, Whitby, Ontario L1N 9B6, Canada. Telephone: 905 430 5000. Fax: 905 430 5020.

Long renowned as the authoritative source for self-guided learning – with more than 40 million copies sold worldwide – the **teach yourself** series includes over 300 titles in the fields of languages, crafts, hobbies, business, computing and education.

British Library Cataloguing in Publication Data: a catalogue record for this title is available from the British Library.

Library of Congress Catalog Card Number: on file.

First published in UK 2005 by Hodder Arnold, 338 Euston Road, London, NW1 3BH.

First published in US 2005 by Contemporary Books, a Division of the McGraw-Hill Companies, 1 Prudential Plaza, 130 East Randolph Street, Chicago, IL 60601 USA.

This edition published 2005.

Typeset by Transet Limited, Coventry, England.
Printed in Great Britain for Hodder Arnold, a division of Hodder Headline, 338 Euston Road, London NW1 3BH, by Cox & Wyman Ltd, Reading, Berkshire.

Hodder Headline's policy is to use papers that are natural, renewable and recyclable products and made from wood grown in sustainable forests. The logging and manufacturing processes are expected to conform to the environmental regulations of the country of origin.

Impression number 10 9 8 7 6 5 4 3 2 1
Year 2009 2008 2007 2006 2005 2004

contents

	introduction	**1**
01	**developing your training strategy**	**3**
	what is training?	4
	why do you need to train?	4
	work and learning have changed	7
	training needs analysis	8
	what do you want to achieve?	13
	an organized approach to training	15
	summary	15
	revision test	15
02	**what type of training?**	**17**
	assess what's available	18
	courses and seminars	18
	formal qualifications	21
	technology	22
	induction training	26
	less formal methods	26
	summary	28
	revision test	29
03	**in-house training methods**	**30**
	induction training	31
	on-the-job instruction	32
	coaching	34
	communication	35
	job manuals	37
	mentoring	38
	focused projects	39
	summary	40
	revision test	41
04	**deciding which course**	**42**
	importance of setting aims and objectives	43
	costs and benefits	45

	what is a good training course?	46
	internal or external training solutions	48
	choosing an external course	49
	training providers	50
	self-assessment – could you be a trainer?	52
	summary	54
	revision test	54
05	**becoming a trainer – preparation**	**55**
	preparation	56
	how important is preparation?	57
	know your audience	57
	know your environment	59
	creating notes that work	61
	summary	62
	revision test	63
06	**designing a course**	**64**
	a balanced structure	65
	content	70
	the importance of timing	73
	what presentation skills do you need?	75
	creating a good learning environment	76
	summary	78
	revision test	79
07	**delivery**	**80**
	that all-important first impression	81
	what is a good presentation?	82
	how to keep the session alive	84
	body language	85
	discussion – should you lead it or follow it?	87
	dealing with questions	89
	summary	91
	revision test	91
08	**visual aids**	**93**
	different types	94
	when to use them and when not to…	99
	top tips for preparing visual aids	100
	summary	101
	revision test	102
09	**dealing with different learning types**	**103**
	different learning styles	104
	keeping your goals in sight	107

hecklers, know-it-alls and talkative types 108
the shy, the anxious and the overwhelmed 109
the uninterested 109
summary 111
revision test 111
10 **evaluation during the session** **112**
why evaluate? 113
appropriate questioning 113
setting exercises and action plans 115
giving and receiving feedback 117
revision test 120
ending the session 120
an event questionnaire and how to use the results 122
summary 125
revision test 126
11 **evaluating after training** **127**
the importance of evaluating any training 128
cost-effectiveness 130
following up with individuals 132
following up with customers 136
presenting your results 137
summary 138
revision test 139
conclusion **140**
taking it further **142**
useful reading 142
useful organizations and websites 142
revision test answers **144**
index **149**

Acknowledgements

Thank you to all the helpful people at Hodder & Stoughton and to my husband Bill for his faith and encouragement.

Dedication

This book is dedicated to the cancer teams at Leighton Hospital, Crewe and Christie Hospital, Manchester.

1 introduction

In this book you will:

- get an overview of training and find out how you can decide what training will help your organization
- find out whether your ideal training solution can be provided in-house or whether you should source it externally
- learn how to design and deliver a training event
- discover how to evaluate training

This book is aimed at managers who have been given responsibility for training and who need an overview of the whole subject so that they can assess the training needs within their organization and then choose the appropriate solution.

We will look at what benefits you should expect from your training, the different types of training that are available (both from external providers and in-house provision) and how to design and deliver an internal course including the use of visual aids to enhance presentation. We will also see how to evaluate the results of the training both during a training event and after so that you will be able to assess its effectiveness. Along the way, we will look at the presentation skills that you need to be able to deliver a course or seminar and also meet some of the learning types that you may come across on your journey towards becoming a trainer. There will be lots of tips on topics such as presentation and creating visual aids plus sample forms for course assessment, revision tests and self-assessment.

The very first chapter will introduce you to the important topic of analysing the training needs of your organization and will help you to make the decisions necessary to use training to move the business forward. Later in the book we will look at the choices available to you regarding your training solutions – including coaching, mentoring, on-the-job instruction and induction training. After a look at running an in-house training event, we will find out the methods by which you can evaluate the success of any training given.

developing your training strategy

In this chapter you will:

- **find out why your organization needs a training strategy**
- **learn how to evaluate the training needs of your company and its staff**

What is training?

Training is the formal teaching of skills and is often undertaken by an organization as a strategic activity aimed at improving the performance of the business by improving the performance of its employees. A training course or seminar or other type of training event is an experience designed to impart knowledge and/or skills.

Why do you need to train?

Training – the act of changing behaviour and attitudes by imparting knowledge and skills – is an essential part of the strategy of any organization that wants or needs to move forwards. It is a way of helping to change the way a business works and of making sure that all its employees perform to the best of their abilities. However, deciding what training will benefit your organization is a far from simple process. It is not possible – because of financial and time constraints – to offer training to all staff willy-nilly. It must be a considered decision taken with the current and future needs of the company in mind.

The first action you should take in deciding what, if any, training is necessary in your organization is to evaluate your business. Perhaps things are going well. It's profitable, no major problems and you have big plans for the future. But do you know how you're going to get to where you want to be? And are you sure that you have the people around you to help you to realize your dream? Maybe everything is OK and you have no desire to change. If so, you may well find that change will be forced upon you and training will become a necessity. If you are not absolutely sure that the people in your organization have all the qualities, skills and capabilities that are vital to your business, then you definitely need to review your training needs. You should also ask yourself whether all your current staff – who may be perfectly equipped to help you in your business – would be happy to stay in an organization where they are not being stretched and developed. Don't forget that training can be motivational and can help with staff retention.

On the other hand, you might already have identified serious problems within your business. You may be losing money, or staff may be leaving to go to other, more forward-thinking companies. You may have customer service issues that you are finding difficult to resolve or cash-flow problems. If you are in this situation, then you can be sure that some – or maybe all of your staff – do not have the appropriate skills to deal with the issues in your business. Without the right skills, it will be impossible for your business to remain – or become – competitive. You need to train and develop your people and your next move must be to work out what they, and your business, need.

Over recent years, more and more businesses have recognized that their people are their most precious resource. Good, well-trained staff can make the difference between a great profit and a catastrophic loss. The temptation, of course, is to put it off. Some managers will always insist that there just is not the time to deal with training. This is a mistaken assumption as it may be that with the properly trained staff performing well, the tasks will get done more quickly. It is certainly true that undertrained staff will not be working to the best of their ability and the company that employs them will not have an easy time reaching its goals. Another objection to training that is often raised is that any training that the company may invest in will be wasted if people do not stay with the organization. The argument against this is to look at it from a different angle. If you do not train your staff, what will happen if they stay? An organization that does not train its workforce so that it can meet the challenges in today's aggressive markets will not survive. To do more than merely survive, you need to gain and maintain a competitive edge by ensuring that your staff are the best they can be for your business.

One area where all businesses can improve is communication. 'Improving our communication' is an objective stated by so many organizations (and so often!) as one of their prime goals, that it has now become almost a cliché. Nevertheless it is an aim that is valid for all companies. Bad communication practices (perhaps where a company keeps its personnel in the dark and eventually loses its best workers or, for example, where an organization does not know how to limit damage caused by customer complaints) can ruin businesses. Conversely, good communication (where businesses tell staff the good news and the bad in just the right way, or perhaps where they turn customer complaints into sales opportunities) can turn a company's fortunes around. Training can help to improve communication within an organization.

Raising the profile of training within an organization can be achieved by a variety of means, all of which involve management commitment and, above all, communication. If the people within an organization are to be fully committed to improving their performance and also to be convinced that training will help them to do this, then developing a training culture is vital. A training culture is one that takes training seriously and devotes sufficient time and resources to it. Some of the instruments that can be used to build training into the culture of a business are:

- notice boards – use these consistently for calls for candidates for special training initiatives or for announcing successes
- newsletters – use these to publicize forthcoming training initiatives or individual successes in training
- staff appraisal procedures – assessing individual training needs and also soliciting ideas about future training needs
- all internal communications such as memos, reports and e-mails – these should always be used to raise the profile of training within the organization
- debriefings after training events – this could include a trainee reporting back to his line manager
- post-course evaluation forms – these will not just provide the company with information about the effectiveness of the training, but can also reinforce the learning and remind the delegates of the course objectives
- meetings – departmental meetings can be used to discuss the skills available among the staff and to decide what additional skills would assist the department in meeting its goals or to practise newly acquired presentational skills

Communication can be both a training need and a training tool. We will look at communication improvements as a training requirement in the training needs analysis section later in this chapter, and will refer to communication as a training tool in the section on types of training in Chapter 2. For now, it is sufficient to say that anyone with responsibility for training of staff should place communication high up on their list of priorities.

A further compelling reason for training and developing staff will be explored in the next section where we will look at how the world of work has changed. Change is an ever-present threat to business and we must continually improve in all areas so that we can avoid the situation where change overtakes us and makes our businesses less competitive. But before we look at change in detail, let's sum up the reasons for training your staff:

- to gain a competitive advantage
- to increase staff motivation
- to extend or fine-tune existing skills

- to improve communication
- to deal with changes in the business
- to use new technology
- to increase flexibility
- to improve staff retention
- to decrease absenteeism
- to change attitudes

> **TRAINING TIP**
>
> Don't let anyone persuade you that training isn't crucial to an organization. Remember, if you think training is expensive, try ignorance!

Work and learning have changed

Change is constant. Throughout the world in the past few decades we have seen major political, social and technological changes and many of the developments in these areas affect the world of work. Business changes drive the need for training. For example, technological advances may lead to the introduction of a new manufacturing process which, in turn, will lead to a need for companies to organize training for their workforce to keep up with the new technology. Commercial and social changes may lead to a demand for higher quality of service in retail businesses, producing a need for customer service training.

Some of the enormous changes that have occurred in the last few decades include:

- computers now control machines in many factories and workshops
- PCs are now in all offices and workplaces – managers type their own letters and reports
- PCs and networks are now more powerful than would have been believed possible even thirty years ago
- the World Wide Web – the world's most powerful network – has revolutionized many areas of business and training
- apprenticeships are less common in some work areas and shorter training courses are more prevalent
- many more people work from home
- there is more career mobility – today's workers do not expect to have the same job from leaving school until retirement

The implications of these changes for training are enormous. Take just one example of changing training needs – most workers now in their fifties would not have even seen a computer while they were still in full-time education but many of them now need to use them on a day-to-day basis. Because they will not have received even rudimentary computer training at school, they will all need training while at work.

Changes in the working world mean changes must be made in the training that is given and also in how it is delivered. Technology is increasingly being used to deliver training – via PCs using software packages or online using the internet.

Training needs analysis

It is vital that you conduct a training needs analysis before setting up any training plans. It would be unwise to commit yourself to any of the costs or effort associated with training before considering what your organization needs and what skills and aptitudes are already available. You must identify the gap (and there probably will be a gap) between what the organization requires to carry out its business plan – now and in the future – and what all the individuals are able to deliver in their various roles.

How will you identify that such a gap exists? There are several telltale signs that training is necessary within your organization. These could include:

- repeated mistakes in any area
- a growing number of accidents
- lack of an adequate induction programme for new recruits
- complaints – these can be from customers, suppliers or from within your organization
- high recruitment costs resulting from a high staff turnover
- conflict between members of your team
- issues raised at exit interviews or staff appraisals
- absenteeism
- requests for training from staff members or workers' representatives
- poor trading performance without adequate explanation
- incentive bonuses not achieved
- poor communication practices – these could be highlighted by your staff, your customers or your suppliers

In addition, external influences can create an extra training requirement. These might include:

- changes in practice in your business area
- new legislation with training implications
- a new piece of machinery
- a new computer system or piece of software

If any of the above signs are found, then several actions must be taken to specify where the skills gap has occurred and what appropriate actions might be necessary to fill it. A baseline of measures to evaluate and assess not only the staff but also the organization must be put into place:

- a comprehensive staff appraisal scheme – if one is not already in operation
- job descriptions for each position
- person specifications for each member of staff
- organization targets – for profits and sales or output as well as administrative targets for potential problems such as absenteeism and high staff turnover
- individual objectives
- a mission statement

In short, you must know your business. You must also be able to show that any training need that you identify during your training needs analysis (and also any request for training that you may receive from anyone within your organization) can be linked to a specific business need.

Before you set up any training in-house or buy training courses externally, you need to evaluate all areas of your organization so that you know exactly what you are trying to achieve. You need to understand where your organization is going (the organizational goals) and also how it is going to get there (the performance needed to reach those goals). Much of the information you require will be readily available but some may need to have a system put in place to obtain it. For instance, you may already have job descriptions but not person specifications or you may never have thought of developing a mission statement. Wherever you find the gap in your information about your business, you will have to fill the gap. During your search for all this information you will undoubtedly find out a lot about the training needs that exist in your organization. This will allow you to take the next step in assessing the needs of the company and of the individual members of staff.

The needs of the company in training terms will become apparent when you know the organizational goals and the performance needed to reach those goals. The gap between current performance and required performance is the one that you will have to fill with the help of your training solutions. So if, for example, one of the goals involves increasing sales by 50 per cent and the current performance of the sales team is static year on year, you will know that some training for the sales team and/or the sales management is something to which you should give serious consideration.

During your training needs analysis you should pay particular attention to the standard of communications within your organization. You can get a feel for this yourself during your fact-finding by asking yourself a few questions:

- is information easy to get hold of?
- do people talk freely about their jobs and their aspirations?
- do your bosses give you the information and assistance you need to get the job done?

You may also develop questionnaires to help you assess the state of your organization's policy and practice of communication. These could be sent to members of staff, suppliers and customers. If you do not have sufficient time to accomplish this yourself, don't forget that (if you have the budget) there are specialist companies that will carry out this type of research for you.

As you can see, conducting a training needs analysis involves gaining a thorough knowledge of the organization – the changes that are affecting it, the management of those changes, the problems the business faces, the aptitudes and attitudes of its personnel – and then designing the solutions. It is not a job for the fainthearted and will need very careful management. But, with determination and an organized approach, it is an achievable and satisfying task. The various elements of the project must be managed including:

- gathering all the relevant information – including conducting interviews and devising questionnaires
- managing the expectations of the people demanding training
- time management – all the phases will have to be co-ordinated and deadlines met
- setting up and running the necessary meetings
- liaising with people at all levels of the organization
- management of resources
- evaluation of training solutions

Having obtained your baseline data – the organizational targets, current performance figures, job descriptions and so on – you will then need to look at the personnel available to fulfil the organization's goals. This can be carried out in a number of ways:

Interviews – with staff and their managers – to establish whether the skills and knowledge required to do the job (both now and in the future) are present in the work force. You will find out which members of staff are open to learning opportunities and which are not and which departments have needs that can be met by training events. By interviewing not just the staff but also their managers you will ensure a more balanced view so that you avoid subjective statements influencing your decisions.

Questionnaires – these can be circulated both internally and externally. The internal ones will show you where problems exist within your organization and where skills and knowledge are insufficient for effective working. The external ones – if you are able to carry these out without causing any adverse reactions in customers and suppliers – may give you a picture of some of your organization's failings and successes so that you can pinpoint urgent training needs.

Personnel records – these will include absentee rates (by department and by individual if possible), disciplinary and accident records to highlight problems that may be overcome – or at least improved – with training.

Training records – what training have the personnel had in the past? Has it worked? (and if not, why not?) Has the training budget been concentrated in any particular areas? What was the purpose of the training given and were the goals achieved? Is there a requirement for training to reinforce previous training? Are there departments or areas of the business that have completely ignored any training opportunities?

Assessment of prior learning – this process is linked with NVQs but would be a valuable addition to any training needs analysis. In the NVQ process this is carried out before any training is decided upon, as it looks at what the potential trainee can do (rather than what knowledge they have). An assessment of prior learning (APL) can be carried out using a variety of methods including interviews, tests, references from the trainee's managers, log books kept by the trainee and samples of their work. This evaluation of the skills available in the workforce will show you where the gap occurs between what the company wants to achieve and what is actually possible with the current level of training and aptitudes. Filling this gap will be the purpose of any training that you decide needs to be carried out.

During your training needs analysis you will probably identify a number of different training requirements. For example, if the company's strategy involves increasing sales, you will need to see if you have the number of appropriately skilled sales staff to achieve this. Is the sales force stretched to the limit? If so, the solution may be to employ additional staff. Or could the existing sales force benefit from training that would enhance their sales and achieve the targets that way? If so, then you will need to search out the best way to train them. Another example would be if you identify a problem in a manufacturing area that involves a high number of rejected products. If this is found to be due to misuse of the manufacturing machinery then practical training specific to that machine may be necessary. A third type of training need that you may uncover is where you see a need to change the culture of the company – to encourage better team working, for example – or to change attitudes in a particular department.

Having found your main training needs you must then attempt to prioritize them. This is a far from easy task and you should not allow yourself to be persuaded to deviate from the most important aspect – the organizational goals. At the top of the list should be the training solution that is both urgent and important – it must make a difference now! Further down your list of priorities will come the things that are merely desirable rather than essential.

One more thing to remember, during your training needs analysis, is that you will have contact with different departments and managers throughout your organization and you should ensure that you do not miss an opportunity to further your project. Make sure that you use this opportunity to gain support within your organization for the new training strategy. Use your enthusiasm for the project to bring people along with you as they see the possible benefits of a well-trained workforce. This will be very useful when you are discussing a budget for the training that you have decided upon and also when you are evaluating the effectiveness of the training after it has been delivered.

Your next step is to compare the needs you have identified with what the business wants to achieve.

What do you want to achieve?

Even after you have identified problems within your organization and have conducted a thorough assessment of gaps in your company, it is still possible that training is not the solution. Do not be tempted to set up or purchase a training course for the wrong reasons. Training carried out for the wrong reasons will not solve your problems, nor will it make you a better manager simply for having given your staff some training opportunities. If you waste money on the wrong course or training for the wrong staff, you will merely increase your problems – so make sure you know why you have opted for the training.

Maybe some of your people are in the wrong role – match up the person currently doing the job with the person specification and the job description. Are they ideally suited or, at the very least, capable of doing the job in question? A good test of this last scenario is to imagine that their lives were threatened – would your staff be able to do their jobs to the required standard if their lives depended on it? If the answer is yes, then obviously the problem is not that they do not have the knowledge or capabilities. It is that the workers are not managed correctly. Then you will need to review the training needs and abilities of your managers rather than their subordinates. Another alternative is that a product or service that you are trying to produce but with which you have had problems is not the right product for you in your current circumstances. Is there something else that you could produce with the facilities, equipment and staff you have? Or a change that you could make that would be more effective – and less expensive – than your present methods. Any of these alternatives might mean that extensive training is not necessary.

If, after seriously questioning your problems, motives and information, you decide that training is definitely part of your solution, then you must continue your fact-finding. Ask yourself: what do you want your trainees to be able to do, feel or know that is different from their current situation? You must feel that the training that you choose will result in an outcome that will be the same as the answer to this question.

Quite often finding out what training specific members of your staff need is easy – you could ask them what training they think they need! They will usually know very well what is causing them problems in their current role or will know what they need to learn to progress further in the organization. They may simply confirm your findings (note that this does not mean that you can get by without a full training needs analysis – that might result in training that your staff find very attractive but which is utterly useless to your business) or they may come up with things that you had not thought of but which you can see would be effective and helpful. Whichever result you get from such a consultation, it will have been a useful exercise.

After this you will arrive at a list of objectives for your training that will state what you want, and are able, to achieve. As always, your objectives must be:

- **Measurable** – decide how to quantify the improvement you want to see after the training has taken place. For example, if you think that a training course for your customer services staff is necessary, set a target for reduction in the number of customer complaints or returned goods or an increase in sales totals in a specific area – whatever fits your business.
- **Possible** – can you afford the training that you are proposing? Will you be able to release the relevant staff for the amount of time that the proposed training will take? Will the nominated staff be able to cope with the level of course?
- **Positive** – remember that all goals and objectives must be stated positively. Your training objectives should encapsulate the goals that you have arrived at during your training needs analysis. Make sure you write them down and keep them in front of you during any associated work that you do, as they will help to keep you on track. Do remember that your training objectives must support the commercial objectives of your organization. The primary purpose of a training strategy is to improve the performance of the business and should not be put into place simply to further individual development – even though this is a welcome by-product of training.

One more thing to remember about training strategies and objectives – they will need updating regularly. If the direction, size or culture of the organization changes, or the environment in which it is operating, then the training plans will need to be amended accordingly. In any event, the strategy should be reviewed on a regular basis so that you can be sure that the training plans will still work to improve the performance of the business in the right way.

An organized approach to training

It is imperative that you take an organized, step-by-step approach to training:

1 Review the needs of the organization.
2 Assess the current capabilities.
3 Prioritize the training needs.
4 Set learning objectives for each training event.
5 Design or purchase an appropriate training event.
6 Deliver the training, evaluating during the event.
7 Implement the training in the workplace.
8 Evaluate the change made as a result of the training.
9 Continue to review the needs of the organization.

Summary

Your training decisions must be based upon:

- the aims and objectives for the future of the organization
- carefully gathered information about both the company and the individual employees
- ensuring that good staff can be developed to avoid losing them to the competition
- specific benefits that you want to gain for your company
- clearly stated training objectives

Revision test

1 What is the first step you should take in deciding what training is necessary in your organization?
2 Name three areas that can be improved by training.
3 What sort of analysis would you have to carry out to identify the gap between what your organization requires and what its individuals are able to deliver?
4 Questionnaires can be useful during a training needs analysis. Who might you send these to?
5 Name three methods of assessing prior learning.
6 Which training solution should be at the top of your priority list?

7 Name an easy way to find out what training specific members of staff need.
8 How might you measure the improvement following a training course for customer service staff?
9 What is the primary purpose of a training strategy?
10 What is the main reason for developing valuable staff?

02 what type of training?

In this chapter you will:

- **learn what factors will influence your choice of training medium**
- **assess the different ways of delivering training**

Assess what's available

Having decided that your business and your staff are in need of training in at least one area, your next move should be to assess the various types of training methods available and their suitability for the training need. Some subjects are so wide that a formal course with a qualification at the end of it is the only way to do it justice. Other topics for which you may have identified a training need may be very specialized – a new piece of in-house software, for example, that is not being used to its full potential – so that a question-and-answer session involving all the relevant personnel may be the ideal solution to the problem. The type of training that you decide upon must fit the need that you have identified, as well as the individual. Here is a list of the things that you should look out for when deciding upon the type of training. It should be:

- effective – you should be convinced that it will meet your objectives
- cost-effective – it should not just be the cheapest, but the best training available taking into account the cost; you must remember that you will have to justify the costs
- appropriate – it must suit the needs of the trainee
- positive – you need to look for opportunities to motivate staff
- timely – it should be available at the right time and be a productive use of the time available
- available – the resources (including budget, personnel and facilities) should be readily available

Obviously, this list of requirements can be met to a greater or lesser degree in individual circumstances by a variety of methods (and by a combination of the available methods) and we will now look briefly at the main ones.

Courses and seminars

The first thing to remember about courses is that they are not the only solution to training needs. Many people hold the belief that training is easy – that's the 'just send 'em on a course' approach. But, as you will know if you have been giving the training needs of your organization some serious thought, there is far more to it than that. As you will see from the options described in this chapter, the training solution must be carefully chosen to meet the needs of the business, taking into account the following:

Needs and restrictions of the organization

- budget – a tight budget might dictate that an internal solution (such as on-the-job training or coaching) be found
- time available – if you can only spare the trainee for a day or two, there is no point in looking at a week-long course
- urgency – how quickly do you need to see results from the training? If you have an expensive machine standing idle then you may need to get the operative trained within days, so you will not have time to design and develop a course yourself
- training objective – what do you want to achieve and will the course or other training solution ensure that you meet that objective?
- subject matter – is it an ongoing business need that can be dealt with in-house or something that will be adequately and cost-effectively served by an external training provider?

Needs and restrictions of the individual

- aptitudes – what does the trainee already know? What is their level of education? Asking yourself these two questions will ensure that you find a training solution that neither over- nor underestimates the delegate
- time available – is the trainee prepared to make a commitment to regular training outside working hours, for example?
- future development plans – any training should form part of an overall plan to develop the individual for the future benefit of the business

If you decide that a course is the most appropriate form of training, courses can be purchased externally or designed and run in-house and both of these options have their own advantages and disadvantages.

One obvious drawback of opting for an external course is the cost. Even one-day courses can be very expensive and you must be convinced that, adding the cost of the course to the costs associated with taking an individual away from the business for the duration of the course, the end result will be worth it. An alternative is to run your own course – more of this later – but here we will look at the sorts of training needs that may be met by using a course provided by an external source. These can be broken down into two categories – those that build and refine skills and those that develop managers.

Skills courses

Skills courses can cover an enormous variety of subjects and are usually aimed at a more basic level of experience and education in the workplace. So in this category you will find training courses being offered at local colleges covering practical skills such as joinery, warehousing, engineering, computing and childcare, and will include NVQs (National Vocational Qualifications), Modern Apprenticeships and many certificated short courses. There will also be a range of courses available to ensure efficient use of popular computer software such as word processing and spreadsheets. There will be a variety of offerings locally that include attending regularly full time or part time, on day release or in the trainee's own time in the evenings as well as one-off courses.

The training objectives for these courses will be clearly defined – to bring the trainee up to a standard in a specific skill. If you decide that this is the appropriate route for the training you have in mind, staff at the college or other course provider will be pleased to help you to decide upon the right level of course for the individual trainee.

Management courses

The choice for provision of courses aimed at developing junior and middle management is often wider but more expensive. You will still find an enormous amount of public provision – by local colleges, universities and training organizations – but there will also be offerings by freelance training consultants, management colleges and other commercial providers.

In this category you will find everything from a one-day course on delegation or sales techniques – including a mixture of presentations, role-play sessions and exercises – to an MBA course lasting a year or more.

The preliminary training objective for management courses may well be less clearly stated – 'to develop the management potential of a junior manager' for example, but each element of the training that you are providing must, nevertheless, have a specific aim. In the case of a junior sales representative you may choose a course on negotiating skills followed by training in sales management with the specific aim of the trainee reaching the level of expertise where he can negotiate at a senior level and manage a sales force of twenty. In this way you will have a development path worked out.

As you can see, courses in both the skills and management categories can include ones where a formal qualification is awarded and these are also the subject of our next section.

Formal qualifications

Courses where delegates can gain formal qualifications are, by definition, external, and often longer than the types of courses usually considered to cater for immediate business needs. Embarking on a long course of study, with the backing and support of their employer, can be very motivating for many people and can increase the loyalty that the employee feels towards the business. This sort of course is frequently viewed – by both the trainee and the employer – as an investment in the individual's future.

The providers of courses leading to formal qualifications can range from the local college, where attendance can be required on a part-time basis over a number of years, to distance learning organizations offering courses by correspondence or online or by a combination of methods. Courses leading to formal qualifications would include the public sector provision (for example NVQs) offered by colleges and the wide variety of courses (including degree and diploma courses) offered by the Open University.

The choice of provider will largely depend upon:

- the educational level of the trainee
- the type of course that is deemed suitable to meet the training objective
- cost
- the time available to be spent on getting the qualification
- whether or not the employer is prepared to back the trainee, not just with financial help towards the cost of the course but also with the time away from work that will be necessary for some courses

Developing employees through encouragement of – or even insistence upon – their participation in courses leading to formal qualifications can be very rewarding for an organization. The benefits can include:

- **Experience** – many courses include work that directly relates to the trainee's day-to-day work. For example, a trainee working towards an NVQ must compile a portfolio of evidence of the type and level of work that they have undertaken. They must do the work and provide proof of its standard before they can be considered for the award of the qualification. The benefit of the experience arising from participation in a course of study can also be something that will be useful in the future. The example of a student on a management course would illustrate this. The trainee may be at a junior level in your organization while he is gaining the qualification but during the course will be exposed to a level of decision making processes that he will need to put into practice when he attains a more senior level in your company.

- **Knowledge** – this is one of the most important, and obvious, things that you are hoping the trainee gains from the course of study.
- **Networking** – mixing with people from other organizations can provide benefits for both the trainee and their organization.
- **Motivation** – when a member of staff obtains a formal qualification with the backing of their employer, there may well be a 'ripple effect' throughout the organization. Not only the successful student but also his colleagues will feel better about themselves and about the company. The benefits of this should be obvious – motivated staff usually work harder, are more effective and, quite often, are more loyal to their employer. Staff motivation and retention is an important benefit of a successful training policy.

Technology

In recent years the way that training is delivered has been revolutionized by new technology and the possibilities that have been opened up by technological developments such as the increased processing power of personal computers and the spread of computer networks (including the internet – the largest, most powerful network in the world) are enormous. Conventional, face-to-face, classroom-based training is still very popular, and is unlikely to be replaced completely, but many people are learning new skills using the World Wide Web for online courses, or CDs/DVDs for learning on computer. This revolution in learning has been termed e-learning and the term refers to any learning that is facilitated by electronic technology. Of course, any of the newer media can be combined with the older ways of learning to suit the subject and the learner. For example, some correspondence courses will deliver many modules using written materials and then supplement these with CDs and may also add in some face-to-face tuition or some testing and reinforcement carried out via computer-based modules. The Open University was one of the first major learning providers to fully embrace this way of combining the different ways of learning. Their courses involve written presentations, books, television broadcasts, e-mail groups, face-to-face tutorials, videos, assignments marked by a tutor and assignments marked by computer.

Taking the personal computer as the starting point for using many of the new technologies, there are two main ways that learning can be facilitated. Firstly, instruction on a variety of topics can be delivered using the computer in a self-contained way. This is especially suited where the learning objectives are clearly defined and, perhaps, limited and would include interactive tutorials (for example typing tutorials) or problem-solving exercises.

Moving on to where information and communications technology (ICT) is used, lessons of many types can be delivered using e-mail or by logging on to a website and using a password to gain access to interactive learning. In this method, the learner can also keep in touch with other students or a tutor via e-mail. This has the added benefit of allowing feedback during learning whilst allowing the learner to control his own learning environment and pace.

Let's look at these two areas of computer-based learning in a little more detail:

Self-contained learning

Self-contained learning programmes using computer technology usually take the form of CD-ROMs or DVDs. These computer disks can be used by an independent learner with access to a PC with a CD/DVD drive so that they can work at home or at work and at a time to suit the learner and/or his employer. This flexibility often suits today's workplace where it can be difficult to release staff for periods of several days at a time, as the learning can be broken into appropriately sized chunks.

The first CD-ROMs to become available for training purposes mainly covered PC software training, but there is now a much larger choice of courses and skills in the CD-ROM marketplace.

The main advantage of this type of training is that CD-ROMs can contain an enormous amount of data and this will include text that can go into as much detail as necessary, both moving and still graphics, audio content and plenty of opportunity for interactivity. This means that the course can include question-and-answer sessions and can offer the trainee many choices regarding the learning path. The learning can be enhanced by the choices made, as the programme will adapt to the level of skill or knowledge shown by the trainee and will automatically reinforce areas where incorrect answers are given.

TRAINING TIP

Don't forget the interactive training that is often available on standard software packages that you will already have on a PC. These tutorials can be helpful for bringing complete beginners up to speed on using word-processing packages, spreadsheets, etc.

Online learning

If you are using a new training provider for an online training programme, you should ensure that the training has been sufficiently tested before you commit to it as this is a relatively new area and there is a danger that you will waste time and money on a programme that is not right for your organization or that has flaws that are not immediately obvious. Make sure that:

- the course content is appropriate – in terms of both breadth and level
- the programme has been adequately piloted
- the staff that you propose to train using the programme have the required level of computer literacy and prior knowledge of the subject area if that is deemed necessary
- your staff have the commitment to follow the programme through
- your organization (or the member of staff if learning at home) has satisfactory access to a computer (PC or Mac) with sufficient processing power and, of course, internet connection
- the programme includes appropriate evaluation techniques – for example that each section must be mastered before the programme allows the learner to proceed to the next stage
- there is a record kept of the performance of the learner so that progress can be monitored by their manager

- the course has a variety of methods of keeping the learner involved and interested – animation, tests, feedback, graphics, humour, simulations, music and video
- the course is easy to navigate

The UK government has set up an agency – learndirect – for the provision and online delivery of courses. The agency offers a wide range of courses ranging from basic IT skills for the absolute computer novice, through specialist IT training and business, languages and management courses, to word and number skills. These courses can be purchased online and use technology to offer flexibility (learning can be carried out at home, work or at one of learndirect's specially equipped centres) alongside the availability of tutors that can be contacted by e-mail or by going to a learndirect centre as well as the use of workbooks, CD-ROMs and videos. (See the Taking it Further section for contact details.)

Improvements in technology have undoubtedly led to enormous advances in training and are an invaluable aid to many managers trying to organize training while keeping their eye on very tight budgets and working with the minimum of staff. However, as with all types of training, computer-based training does not solve all a trainer's problems. Let's look at the advantages and disadvantages:

Advantages

- learners can set their own pace
- most learning software offers immediate feedback and reinforcement
- the packages can make good use of the capacity for video and audio, animated sequences, graphics, colour and print facilities
- as technology advances, costs are generally decreasing
- flexibility – trainees (or their employer) can choose when and where to carry out the learning
- computers can be used to increase computer literacy
- multimedia approaches to training can be very successful as they engage the senses of seeing and hearing in addition to doing
- the prompt feedback from trainers that is possible using e-mail can motivate learners far more than the delay associated with postal feedback on a traditional distance learning course

Disadvantages

- self-contained learning demands a high degree of self-discipline
- your learners – or your organization – may not be ready to use new technology for training purposes
- learning alone with a computer rules out the development that is possible from interacting with fellow trainees
- not everyone is computer literate so some courses are impossible for them to take
- not everyone has suitable access to a computer
- the learner may not have access to a trainer to whom they can address their questions
- keeping up with advances in technology (always trying to have the latest version of software or the most powerful PC available) can be very expensive and time-consuming
- self-directed learning may produce variable results depending on how motivated the learner is; there will not be a trainer who can assess their progress during the course – this might result in the need to put in place a coaching programme following the completion of the course so that the level of understanding can be gauged and to ensure that the learner is capable of applying their new knowledge and skills.

Induction training

Induction training is an essential part of any organization's training strategy and must be given to any new employee. Poor initial training can lead to chaos: the new starter will feel lost and demotivated; existing employees may become frustrated and annoyed by the new employee's lack of knowledge and self-sufficiency; serious mistakes may be made and several vital matters of 'housekeeping', such as health and safety issues, may be overlooked – with dire consequences.

Less formal methods

There are several methods of training that, although informal, can be just as effective as courses and may also be more cost-effective. However, just because the method of delivery is informal, it does not follow that you can get away without setting objectives for the training or getting it organized to make it effective. There are several distinct methods in this category and we can look briefly at them one-by-one:

Coaching

Coaching differs from instruction in that it involves frequent intervention while allowing the person receiving the coaching to develop within the job. The coach is not there to train someone in new skills but to help to correct the application of skills that already exist. They can then identify any problems in the way in which the work is being carried out and help to improve performance.

On-the-job instruction

This method is employed, often with good results, for both new and experienced employees. With new employees, of course, it will also form part of the induction process, but with existing staff it can be part of their ongoing development within the job and within the company.

Again, this needs to be carefully organized and monitored, with objectives set just as for any other type of training. This method must not be seen as a 'cheap and cheerful' alternative to 'proper training'. Done correctly, by the right person, it can be extremely effective. More on this in the next chapter.

Communication

This is one area that is universally acknowledged as being of prime importance. It is also an area where many organizations fail and, as an element of a company's training strategy, it is often overlooked. You may find, however, that where the majority of your workforce seems to lack a basic understanding of business priorities there will be a breakdown in the organization's methods of communication. This can be remedied by installing – and monitoring – a better communication policy and will be a highly cost-effective way of resolving problems such as this.

Job manuals

When you know that a training task will probably be repeated with new staff, or with existing staff on a regular basis, then it is often worthwhile producing a job manual for future reference. Manuals and checklists (including ones written for a specific task or for a particular position, or manuals supplied with machines or computer software) can also be useful in reinforcing on-the-job instruction or as a starting point for training new staff in a particular task.

Mentoring

Mentoring is where a senior manager takes responsibility for the development of a more junior colleague. Mentoring, like coaching, is not, strictly speaking, training. The job of the mentor is to define the training or other development activities that need to take place in order for the individual to maximize their potential. Their task is not to carry out the training but to identify needs and opportunities.

Focused projects

If you have identified a specific training need in an individual it may be possible to set them a task that will be useful both in fulfilling this training need and also in terms of the company's current work. Properly defined and monitored, projects of this type can provide useful opportunities to extend the scope of a person's abilities.

All of these less formal methods are normally carried out in-house and can be very cost-effective. They will certainly form an important part of any organization's training strategy. We will therefore look in more detail at these methods – along with induction training – in the next chapter.

Summary

- Select the right type of training to suit your requirements – take into account the individual, business needs, budget and time available.
- Courses for practical skills and management topics are available from external providers or can be designed and delivered in-house.
- Less formal methods of training include coaching, on-the-job instruction and mentoring – all of which are carried out in-house.
- Don't forget the use of technology to assist and deliver learning.
- If your organization doesn't already have a successful induction training programme, make that a high priority.

Revision test

1 Name three things that you should take into account when choosing a training solution.
2 How can you be sure that a training solution will suit a trainee's aptitudes?
3 In which type of courses are training objectives more clearly defined, skills courses or management courses?
4 Name three benefits of sending employees on courses leading to formal qualifications.
5 What training packages might you already have available as software on your PC?
6 Name two ways that a learner could obtain access to interactive learning.
7 What could an organization do to ensure that trainees can put their new knowledge and skills into practice following computer-based training?
8 How does coaching differ from instruction?
9 To what might you attribute a workforce's lack of a basic understanding of a business's priorities?
10 What is the aim of mentoring?

In this chapter you will:

- **look at the induction training that is vital to your organization**
- **learn about the various methods of training that are usually carried out in-house**

Induction training

As we have said previously, induction training is essential and should automatically be used whenever someone new starts employment with your organization. As it will be used many times, it is worth putting in the time, effort and money to ensure that this training is effective.

Induction training can help an organization in a number of ways. It can motivate new staff by assuring them that they are not just an insignificant part of a large organization and can reassure them that their new employer cares enough about their progress to invest in comprehensive training straightaway. It should also ensure that all staff members are given standard information about the organization that they are joining.

What should the information you give to your new employees include? In deciding this you must bear in mind that induction (or orientation) training is not person-specific, nor must its content be dictated by the job that the new starter has been hired to do. The ideal to aim for – and perhaps this should be one of your first tasks if you are just starting to review training needs – is the development of a uniform programme that can be followed by each and every new recruit. Essentials for this programme include:

- what the company stands for – the mission statement that you found (or developed) during your training needs analysis will help here
- a 'family tree' or organization chart that shows the main managers of the company, where they fit into the bigger picture and what they do
- what the company does – what service or product does it provide?
- the participation – and commitment – of all the senior managers of the organization in developing and delivering the content of the programme
- all the useful – and essential – information that a starter needs to be able to find their way around a new organization
- a chance for the new recruit to ask questions

Even if you already have an induction programme, a useful addition is the 'buddy system'. This, as the name suggests, is where a member of staff – preferably one from the new recruit's department – is allocated to each starter to guide them through their initial period with the company. A buddy for a new starter could be someone senior or junior to them in terms of position, as the only requisites for being a buddy are that they have experience of how the company works, and know where everything is and what everyone does. With this knowledge they can ease the new recruit's passage through the first week or two with the company.

As part of the company-wide induction programme, you must, of course, ensure that housekeeping items are dealt with in the first few days. Some of these will be the same for all new starters – for example, where toilet facilities are, health and safety issues, what facilities are available for breaks, while others are more job- or department-specific items such as who to go to for help on a variety of matters, a run-down on the current work of their department and introductions to their closest work colleagues.

In short, you must ensure that anything that will give useful and practical information to help new arrivals to settle in to the company is covered.

On-the-job instruction

On-the-job training covers all instruction that takes place alongside the trainee's normal duties and responsibilities. Whether the employee is new or has been with the company for many years, on-the-job training must be handled in the right way to ensure that objectives are met. Yes, training objectives are just as important with this type of training as with any other, even though on-the-job instruction might be viewed as being a lot more informal than a training course or seminar for example.

The correct approach is a systematic one. You must develop a number of steps that you can follow in the correct order no matter what the topic is that is being communicated or who the person is who is receiving instruction.

These steps should include:

- **Set a training objective.** What do you want the trainee to be able to do at the end of the instruction? What improvement in their job should you be able to see – and measure?
- **Start the instruction by describing the task.** Mostly this will be done verbally by the instructor, but you may also consider written reinforcement helpful or even necessary. You might use machine manuals or computer software to help get the message across.

- **Demonstrate.** Watching someone who is proficient at a task can be very helpful in learning how to do something. However, it must not be assumed that someone who can do something well is necessarily the right person to show someone else. Anyone with responsibility for the demonstration part of on-the-job training must be able to interact with the trainee and to manage questions in a constructive way. They must be able to check that what they have said and demonstrated has been understood.

  Demonstration is one of the most important parts of on-the-job training so, even if the task involves interpersonal skills, you should always find examples of how the job should be done. In the case of dealing with customer complaints, for example, a trainee could observe an experienced call handler at work (with explanations and the chance to ask questions following each call) but then would also benefit from some role-play type exercises. These could be used as part of the demonstration and also as practice for the trainee.

  The trainer should also bring company policy and practice into the demonstration. For example, if someone is being trained in health and safety procedures, what is the time allowed for accident reporting? And who is the person responsible for following up the procedure?
- **Let them practice.** The instructor should watch the trainees carry out the task for themselves and be available for questioning and reinforcement during this time. Further practice should be allowed without the instructor present so that the trainee can discover possible problems. Before leaving, the instructor should inform the trainee when they will return and where they can be found in case any problems or queries arise in the meantime.
- **Allow time for questions following the practice session** – to and from both the instructor and the trainee. The trainee may need to add to what they have learned from the demonstration and from having tried the task by asking questions of the instructor and having their worries dealt with at this early stage. The instructor will be able to ask questions of the trainee in order to find out whether or not the trainee has understood the process. The person delivering the training should be able to analyse what extra actions might be necessary to ensure that the task has been learned effectively.

- **Reassure the trainee.** Ensure that they know that they are making progress – positive feedback is never wasted. This can make the difference between a pleasant – and successful – learning experience and one that fails to meet its objectives. You should also make sure that they know where to go for help after the instruction has ended
- **Evaluate.** Check that the training has met its objectives. Analyse how the training went by observation and by asking questions of the trainee (but not leading questions) to ascertain just what has been understood and how their behaviour has changed as a result of the training.

Coaching

Having sorted out the initial training for new starters, you can turn your attention to existing staff and how their performance can be improved by the use of training delivered in-house. Coaching can be a very cost-effective way to reinforce training that has already been carried out and also to develop skills and to pass on knowledge. You may be lucky and find that some senior members of your team have experience of coaching, but usually some training in how to coach will be necessary. Properly developed, a coaching programme can be an important part of your training strategy and can be used to reinforce the learning that has taken place.

The arrangements for the coaching should be agreed between you, the trainee and the coach so that everyone is aware of the objectives and how the method will work. This type of training must be ongoing and each coaching opportunity taken up as and when it arises, but it should go without saying that coaching in front of customers is never a good idea.

Before you go ahead with this option, you must be certain that the chosen coach is capable of the style of observation and intervention necessary. The coach should remember that he or she is not an instructor – the training should have been done before the coaching relationship begins – as coaching is about putting the results of training to good use. When people have newly acquired knowledge or skills it is essential for the business and the individual that it is used to best effect as soon as possible. This will ensure that the training is reinforced by day-to-day use and also that the organization benefits from the investment. Coaching is the ideal way to make sure this happens.

When selecting someone as a coach, you should not choose the trainee's manager. This is because coaching is only effective when the coach can be an unbiased observer and also the coach's attention should be focused on the individual rather than on the team. Although the coach does not have to be an expert in the skills being coached, he or she must be able to understand the right application of these skills and be able to observe and analyse the trainee at work.

Communication

Here we will look at ways in which communication can greatly improve the skills of a workforce, improve motivation and help the company – and its staff – to develop.

The most important thing to remember about communication is that it must be two-way. Reviewing the state of communication within your organization is a useful part of your training needs analysis and may reveal previously unsuspected training needs that can be handled in a cost-effective way.

During this review you must ask yourself questions such as:

- Do we listen to our staff?
- Do our people have all the information they need to enable them to do a good job?
- Do we share ideas with them?
- Do we always tell them the good news as well as the bad news?
- Do we expect them to help us to decide the future direction of their department and of the business?
- Do we take their views on training and development into account?
- Do they trust us – and our communications?
- Do we treat them with respect?

In questioning yourself and other managers in your organization in this way, you may discover that some people need to learn a little more about good communication. This could bring about a course in itself. You may also find that the answers dictate the direction of your training and that you need to offer training events that give more opportunities for communication – between managers and junior staff or between members of working teams or between managers of different departments so that their efforts are better co-ordinated.

Almost all training solutions will obviously involve communication but some are better than others for this purpose. When you are using training to improve communication within an organization, try the following three methods:

- **Role-play** exercises give an opportunity to try out the ways that ideas can be communicated and training put into practice.
- **Planned discussion** of a particular issue. This can be staged as a carefully chaired meeting so that everyone who wants to offer an opinion or solution has plenty of opportunity to be heard.
- **Brainstorming** is a technique that can use communication to develop ideas with your workforce. Many managers seek ways to increase creativity, and brainstorming (where you gather members of a team together, give them a task or objective and ask for ideas) is a method of starting the development of a creative culture within the organization. To hold a brainstorming session demands careful handling but it can be very rewarding. Take a group of people (three or four is ideal but the technique will work for up to 15 members) away from their desks or machines, explain your objective (this could be to explore different ways of increasing the throughput on a machine, for example) and ask for ideas from all the participants. Limit self-consciousness by making sure that everyone involved understands that there are to be no comments at all – either positive or negative – until all the ideas have been collected. The ideas should be noted down quickly, without pausing to consider the value of the idea. You might list them on a flipchart or write each one down on a sticky note. Make sure that you have at least one idea from everyone present and move on to the next stage as soon as you have sufficient material. It can be useful to set a time limit for this first stage. If you've written the ideas down on separate pieces of paper, it can be helpful to group them into two or three categories.

  The next stage is a discussion of the ideas. You should lead this so that all suggestions are analysed and the ones with potential are identified for future work. The first session of brainstorming may be difficult. You will need to lead the discussion to a certain extent by questioning – 'Why have we always done it that way?' 'What would happen if we used this suggestion?' – and by not allowing negative feedback.

This technique can result in some new approaches to old tasks and problems and, done regularly, will improve the team's creativity and help them to work together. Of course, making time for this type of session on a regular basis can be difficult initially. Perhaps you could take time from regular team-briefing sessions that you may have held, substituting a written briefing to be read later, thus freeing up time for the team to spend on the brainstorming activities. The results, in terms of the ideas discussed and the culture change that can be brought about will be worth the effort.

Events such as these, specifically aimed at improving communication, can have many benefits for the organization. While teaching personnel at all levels how to communicate, they will also be developing and improving the culture within the company and passing on information at the same time.

Job manuals

Written information such as job manuals can be a very important part of an organization's training procedures, as not only can they be used for specific training needs but they can also be kept in the appropriate department so that they are available whenever there is doubt as to how to handle something. It is worthwhile developing a comprehensive job manual whenever you judge that the particular training task will need to be repeated with various members of staff over a period of time.

In most cases where job manuals can be created for training, there will be a number of distinct steps that must be followed each time and these can be listed, along with explanatory notes and examples of the forms that must be completed if your system has them. The manual could describe the procedures and the checks that are necessary along the way to ensure that the job is completed and objectives met.

A good example of where a job manual could be useful would be how to deal with a customer complaint. An experienced call handler could describe the steps and the systems used, with explanatory notes added as appropriate.

Mentoring

Mentors are partnered with a more junior colleague with whom they build a developmental relationship so that the junior employee can be helped to reach their potential. In order for the relationship to work effectively it is essential that the mentor is not the direct superior of the mentee. Depending on the staff available and the problems identified, a mentoring programme could be developed in one of two ways:

- linking all junior managers with a senior manager
- arranging mentors for only those junior managers who are judged to have exceptional development potential – with time and money being the usual constraining factors, inclusion in the mentoring programme can be limited to those junior managers who can make the most impact on the business; after all, the purpose of investing time and money in such a programme is to improve the performance of the individual and the company

The relationship between the mentor and the mentee is of prime importance and in view of the possible resistance to mentoring, good communication is essential. The person being mentored must understand that the aim of the programme is to increase their value to the company. A good mentoring relationship will also provide a 'sympathetic ear' for the junior manager's work-related problems and could be quite a low-key, informal relationship.

Many company cultures do not allow time or opportunity to discuss problems, and sometimes even admitting to problems is frowned upon. This type of culture can lead to stress-related problems. A well-organized and well-understood mentoring programme can help to overcome these difficulties.

So, what are the qualities required to be a good mentor? Apart from the pre-requisites of seniority and experience within the company, anyone chosen to be a mentor should be capable of developing a relationship based on trust and confidentiality. It is imperative that the person being mentored can discuss any fears or problems with their mentor without the worry that anything will be repeated without their consent. The mentor should also be capable of being impartial. They may discover, for instance, that the junior manager has difficulties with their line manager but the mentor must not take sides and the best way to help in these circumstances is to offer a different point of view.

Although the mentor is there to help the mentee, it must always be remembered that the aim is to increase the value of the junior manager to the company. After a period spent advising and observing the trainee, the mentor should be able to design a development programme for them and to offer them career guidance. On this last point, it is imperative that the mentor is prepared to admit, if it is felt necessary, that development of this particular trainee is not possible within their current organization.

Focused projects

Focused projects are specific tasks – closely monitored – that may ordinarily be outside the job description of the people who have been set them but which can be set as a developmental activity. For example, a junior manager may be perfectly competent in her job on a day-to-day basis but have difficulties when putting things in writing or researching a major project. In this case setting them a focused project that entails relevant research and a final report to be compiled will give the manager the opportunity to develop.

This type of project must be relevant to the manager's job and will usually present more learning opportunities if a competent mentor is appointed to help the trainee. So, if you need to improve the report-writing capabilities of a junior Human Resources Manager, for example, you might devise a project of looking into the staff retention rate within your organization. A more senior manager who has a reputation for producing good written work – not necessarily a manager from the Human Resources department as cross-departmental co-operation can also be furthered by this method – could be appointed as the junior manager's mentor just for the duration of this project.

The mentor should commit to the project and to helping the trainee and make themselves available for regular consultations and updates. It should be made clear at the start that the mentor is to act purely in an advisory capacity and that responsibility and authority as appropriate will be transferred to the mentee – the trainee must do the work! As the areas that people need help in are also quite often those that they do not like to do, they will often put off the start of a project like this so the deadlines must be clearly set and committed to by both the trainee and the mentor.

There is an enormous variety of the types of project that can be used as training opportunities in this way but some examples include:

- sourcing exercises – a trainee could research the suppliers of a specific item such as a component or new machine and then produce a report as to the best (in terms of both price and quality) in the market
- a report on the company's competition – this would increase the trainee's awareness of the company's position in the marketplace
- a report on efficiency in the company – for example, if the company operates several of one type of machine, the trainee may be able to compare machine efficiencies
- creative thinking – for example, ask trainees to suggest ways of increasing profitability
- a customer satisfaction survey that can be devised then analysed by the trainee

Whatever is chosen as the trainee's project, it must be relevant and have carefully specified aims, objectives and timescales. Given these requirements, focused projects can be a very efficient and cost-effective way of developing staff and can produce real benefits for the company.

Summary

- In-house training can be both effective and relatively inexpensive.
- Make induction training a high priority as it not only delivers real training but also helps to ease the new starter into the organization and can prevent problems developing.
- There is a great variety of training methods that can be developed and used in-house. If used correctly and with care, they will form a major and successful part of your training strategy.
- In-house training methods can be used extensively and will further your aim of creating a culture within your organization that is pro-training.
- Combinations of different types of training can be used according to the specific training objectives and situations.

Revision test

1. Name three essentials of an effective induction training programme.
2. Which system provides a member of staff to guide a new recruit?
3. Why would an instructor need to ask questions during and after on-the-job training?
4. What is the most important thing to remember about communication?
5. Name three methods of training to improve communication within an organization.
6. When should you develop a job manual?
7. What sort of problems can be overcome with the use of mentoring?
8. What type of training can be added to focused projects to provide additional training opportunities?
9. Give three examples of focused projects.
10. Induction training should be a high priority. Name three advantages that it delivers.

04 deciding which course

In this chapter you will:

- **look at the factors that make up an effective course**
- **learn how to find and assess training providers**
- **assess whether you could become a trainer**

Importance of setting aims and objectives

You have already set training objectives for your organization and it is equally important to set learning objectives for each training event that you undertake – whether internal or external.

Setting objectives for a training course is vital and one of the most important areas to be addressed to make sure that you get value for money and effectiveness from your training budget. Your learning objectives for each training event must sum up what you want the event to achieve. Try to develop an objective that states – as succinctly as possible – what the delegates are expected to learn or gain from the training and also includes who the training is aimed at. Write your learning objectives down.

An example of an event objective

Here is an example of the objective that could be set for a customer service training event:

CUSTOMER SERVICE TRAINING –
HOW TO MAKE CUSTOMERS HAPPY AND EASIER TO DEAL WITH

Objective
To reduce the number of customer complaints received by 10% in the forthcoming year.

Who will attend
The Customer Service Course will be attended by all the company's customer service clerks and the Customer Service Manager to ensure that they are all trained in up-to-date customer care techniques.

Planned outcome
The delegates to:

- understand the new procedures and techniques
- demonstrate their understanding of the new customer care procedures by taking part in exercises and role-plays

After the training they will be expected to utilize these techniques to decrease the number of complaints received by a minimum of 10 per cent in the forthcoming year.

Keep in mind that objectives should be **SMART**:

S Specific
M Measurable
A Achievable
R Realistic
T Timed

So, for example, faced with a need for an improvement in sales you may set an objective of increasing total sales figures for the company by 5 per cent per year for the next three years. An 'un-SMART' objective for this, by contrast, might be 'to significantly improve sales'. Compare these two objectives. The SMART one ensures that you can demonstrate a definite result from the training – and you know when to expect the result – whereas the 'un-SMART' one would mean the trainers not knowing exactly what they are trying to achieve, and the trainees being dissatisfied because they would not be able to prove what they had achieved.

A further aspect of training that you must not overlook when you are setting objectives and goals is that of evaluation – what happens after the training event. You must ensure that effective evaluation is carried out and that the learning is reinforced in the workplace (more of this in Chapters 10 and 11). Including this aspect in your initial planning will ensure that you keep sight of what your training is meant to achieve.

The final aspect involves the trainees themselves – the training must be relevant for them so they must be central to your objectives. This means that the sessions must be pitched at the right level and that the trainees themselves have the capacity to learn. Remember too that the training can be used as a motivating factor. This last point can cause some confusion. It does not mean that the provision of training should be used as an incentive (training is for the good of the company as well as that of the trainee), but rather that the idea of training should be 'sold' to the workforce. The benefits for them and for the company should be explained and a genuine effort to change the organizational culture must be one of your goals so that trainees become actively involved in the training process. The payoff from this is simple – motivated trainees will learn more easily and the investment will be worthwhile.

Failure to set aims and objectives for training will result in dissatisfaction all round. Demonstrable achievement is a powerful motivating factor in all training for trainers and trainees alike, while funds for future training are more likely to be easier to come by if you can show the benefits that have accrued from your training strategy.

Costs and benefits

As with any business decision, there are both costs and benefits to be considered when deciding which course is appropriate for your needs. Having carried out a comprehensive training needs analysis and set appropriate goals and benefits, the next stage of your training planning process is to weigh the planned benefits against the projected costs. Here's a quick look at some of the items that should appear on your lists of costs and benefits:

Costs

- direct costs of the course – whether run internally or purchased externally, bills and expense claims will be sent to the company, including those for travel, accommodation, course materials, venue costs, trainer's fees, etc.
- delegates' salaries
- loss of the work that the delegates would have done if they had not been attending the course – or the temporary staff to replace them
- cost of the time spent conducting a training needs analysis and preparing or purchasing a training event

Benefits

- training can improve staff retention when it is used to motivate staff and increase their commitment to the organization
- a business problem can be solved with effective training – accident rates or absenteeism may decrease, for example
- profits may increase – sales people may become more effective and sell more goods or sell goods at higher prices after training in negotiation techniques, for example
- manufacturing output may increase thereby decreasing production costs per item
- the number of staff required to do a job may decrease resulting in a reduction in the amount spent on salaries and wages
- staff recruitment may become easier when a company has a reputation as one that is committed to training

- the organization can keep up with developments in technology – and with its competitors – by investing in training
- altruistic benefits may be found – contribution to the community, for example, may be a valuable benefit in some companies

What is a good training course?

The answer to that question is simple – and complicated! Put simply, a good training course is one that meets all your requirements. Viewed in more depth, a good training course is one that will be effective – but defining that effectiveness can be quite difficult. You will need to do a lot of research so that you know what skills you already have within your organization and also that you know what training is available – and at what price – outside your company. When you have done this, you will then be in a position to choose your training. Use the checklist below to help.

Course choice checklist

- Does the course content match the training need that you have identified? Will successful completion of the course enable your delegates to be able to do what you want them to do?
- Will the content keep your delegates interested? If you feel that they may be bored by parts of the material, take care – a bored delegate will not learn much and probably will not ultimately make a more effective employee.
- Is it going to be cost-effective? Will the benefits justify the costs?
- Does the course use the appropriate method of delivery? A course that is very practical and 'hands-on' may not necessarily suit a very academic subject with delegates who are senior managers in your organization. Similarly, a course based on listening and then completing written exercises may not be appropriate for practical skills training, with delegates who feel uncomfortable with written materials.
- Is the venue convenient and suitable? You must take into account possible costs of accommodation and travel as well as the size and layout of the training rooms.
- Is the course the right length? If it is an event of more than a day or two, can the business continue while the delegates are

on the course? Will you have to organize temporary cover for any of the trainee's positions? Is the length appropriate for the subject matter?

- If you are considering an external course, do you know the training provider? If you have had previous, good experiences of the provider you are proposing to use, then you will be able to purchase a course with confidence. If you don't have personal experience of the training provider, do your research carefully.
- Does the course fit in with the culture of your organization? It may be that the training provider in question has a different approach to the subject from that of your business. For example, a course on disciplinary procedures may take a hard line towards minor transgressions. Managers returning from such a course to an organization with a much more lenient view of staff behaviour would find it difficult to put into practice what they have learned. This match between the culture of the organization and the approach of the training is important – unless your aim is to change your organization's culture, of course! In this case, the course will be just one part of your strategy for change.

Of course, any training solution that you decide upon must meet the objectives set for the training at an affordable price. If you have neglected to set specific objectives, then you will be unable to tell whether the training course that you propose is going to be suitable, so read the section about objectives above and make that the very first thing you do after you have gathered all your information about the need for training in your organization. Having set your objectives and obtained sufficient information about the training needs, you will be in a position to differentiate between a good course – one that is good quality and closely matches your needs – and a bad one.

From a delegate's point of view, a successful course is one that is not boring and that teaches them something useful. Obviously only the latter part of this view ties in directly with the objectives of the company paying for the training. However, it is essential that the delegate's needs are taken into account in assessing the effectiveness of a course. It is unlikely that a bored trainee will gain the maximum amount of useable knowledge from any training so the course should be structured so that the delegate's interest is maintained. A good training course will therefore contain a variety of different elements and learning methods.

TRAINING TIP

Ask yourself continually: 'Does this training solution meet my objectives?'

Internal or external training solutions

Most training solutions (with the obvious exceptions of induction training and short courses to demonstrate internal systems or to address issues involving the company culture) can be provided by external sources. However, budget is usually the main limiting factor when deciding whether to purchase your training solution or to develop your own course or seminar. Time constraints will also often help to determine your choice. It may be that you, and other senior managers who would be able to offer valuable input to an internal course, would not be able to devote sufficient time to your project without seriously affecting the running of the business. In this case, choosing an external course would be more appropriate. This is especially true in a small company where there is insufficient cover to keep the business operating at an acceptable level.

Other factors that you should take into account when making the decision include the number of people who need training in one particular area. If there are only one or two people and you are convinced that a course is the right training solution (rather than, perhaps, coaching or on-the-job instruction) then an external course or seminar could well be the answer. Certainly it would be unlikely to be cost-effective for you to run an internal course for a limited number of delegates unless you predict that the materials you develop for the course will be used a number of times in the future.

You should also consider other important advantages of your staff attending an external course. It may be that the contact with other people in your business sector that your delegates would get if they attended an external course in a specialized area will add extra value to the course for them and for your business.

If you are being put off external provision by the knowledge that the course content is generic – applies to many organizations rather than specifically to your own organization's circumstances and needs – then do consider the following possibility. Your staff could attend the external course, gaining the benefits associated with that, and then you could arrange a coaching programme for them when they return to work, designed to convert their newly acquired skills or knowledge into something that is company specific.

In this way you can take advantage of being able to send perhaps one or two people on an external course more cost-effectively than running an internal course. Coaching in the workplace following a course will ensure that the new skills are used appropriately back in the work environment.

Turning now to the in-house option, the main advantage of developing and running your own course is that you are in control. You can decide upon the exact content and style of the course so that it fits your objectives perfectly. You can also determine the length and timing of the training so that it is run at a time that suits your business and is as short – or as long – as your commitments will allow.

The disadvantages are, of course, obvious. The time that it takes to develop and research a worthwhile course may be more than you can spare from your other duties and responsibilities. Also, other senior managers may be reluctant to devote time to presenting some of the important parts of the course you have in mind. You also need to be absolutely certain that you have not just the time to devote to this venture, but also the commitment to see it through. In addition, you must be confident that you can run a course. The questionnaire later in this chapter will help you to assess your aptitudes in this area.

Choosing an external course

Choosing just the right course from among the many hundreds available can be a daunting task. However, if you keep the learning objective in mind and take a systematic approach, the decision can become easier. Here are some things – apart from that all-important objective – to keep in mind:

- **cost** – this is always a factor in deciding what training your organization can offer to its employees and the course you select must represent real value for money to your business
- **the training company** – check out their credentials and try to speak with one or more of their customers
- **number of delegates** – check how many delegates are scheduled; too many could mean that your staff are not given the attention they need (and that you will be paying for)

- **level of participation** – this is tied in with the number of delegates on a course, and needs to suit the type of learning experience that you want to buy for your delegates
- **format** – courses and seminars can last from half a day to a number of years and the format will be governed by the content and the learning objectives

Training providers

Purchasing cost-effective training is just like any other purchasing exercise – you must do your homework. There are many companies offering courses (both ready-made and tailor-made) but some are excellent and some are best avoided. So how do you find the good ones? Recommendation is always a good starting point, but you will still have to check out the provider and ensure that what they are offering meets your needs and will fulfil your objectives.

Checking out training providers can be a long process but is essential if you want to avoid wasted money from your precious training budget and also to avoid discouraged trainees and staff who return to work thinking that they know how to do something but do not have all the knowledge necessary to see the job through successfully. Badly trained staff may also be given duties and responsibilities that they are not ready for. This results in a lack of motivation in both the trainees and their managers and is a poor recommendation for your training strategy.

The first thing to do when looking for new training providers is to gather as much information as possible about what is out there in the training market. Here are some resources:

- Recommendation – ask around. Your colleagues may have attended good courses or some of your contacts in other companies may have relationships with good quality providers.
- Your local Chamber of Commerce and Business Link organizations.
- Check out what is available at your local colleges of Further Education – public provision is often of excellent quality and, if the content is appropriate, can provide a cost-effective training solution.
- Learndirect – they have a national training advice line and also provide many reasonably priced local courses, especially in the IT area.

- Your local council. Their Trading Standards Department can offer advice and may be a training provider themselves. They may offer both standard and tailor-made courses on a variety of topics such as Food Hygiene regulations or other legislation that affects your business.
- The internet – always a good research tool. In addition to finding online training, you will find a lot of information about training and training providers.
- Yellow Pages – but do not make the mistake of thinking that the company with the biggest advertisement is necessarily the best provider (or even the biggest). You should be able to find local freelance trainers who may suit your requirements, but they will still need careful checking.

Checking out suppliers should be a matter of routine, whether they are supplying raw materials, office supplies or training. Measures you should take include:

- asking around – someone you know may have had a bad experience with your proposed supplier
- interviewing the provider – make sure that you are very clear about your objectives for the training so that you can conduct an effective interview
- finding out how much they will charge and how they will charge – some charge a one-off fee per course while others may charge a fee per day and will estimate how long the preparation for the course will take
- reading the provider's literature carefully – and questioning them on it
- seeing them in action if possible
- reviewing the course content in detail – does it meet all your objectives? Does it represent value for money? Will it fit in with your business commitments?

The gap between what is offered in the public sector and the offerings of specialized companies and consultants has narrowed over recent years and the cost of courses offered by public providers such as local colleges may be considerably lower. However, do bear in mind that these courses are often very general in content as they are aimed at a very wide market, so if you need a course that pays specific attention to your industry then you may need to look at specialist trainers or develop your own course.

Self-assessment – could you be a trainer?

You may already have decided, for one of a number of reasons – lack of time, confidence, facilities or expertise perhaps – that you will not be running your own training event. There will be some reading this book who, again for various reasons – lack of money allocated to training, their previous experience of running a course or the desire to broaden their expertise to include this skill, for example – will be giving consideration to planning and running an internal course to meet their specific business need. For this latter group of readers (and perhaps the curious among you in the first group), the self-assessment questionnaire shown in Figure 1 will help you to decide.

In-house provision – start small

If you do decide to try some in-house training, it is a good idea to start small. Even relatively short amounts of time can be put to good use. With organization and discipline, excellent results can be obtained from a regular training session lasting no longer than half an hour.

You will no doubt have seen the notices on shop doors 'Closed on Tuesdays 9.00 to 10.00 a.m. for staff training'. Ever wondered what they do in these short sessions? They probably run through the latest edicts from Head Office on how to use the sales systems that the company employs or discuss the forthcoming cut-price sale requirements. My doctor's surgery has recently designated Wednesday lunchtime as their regular training slot and that is when they learn how to use the technology that controls the appointment system and patients' records.

The point is that this repeated training in short bursts can show results without costing a great deal or over-taxing your presentation skills. It is a good way to break into the world of training.

The main requirement for these short sessions is discipline. You – and your staff – must be prepared to make a commitment to finding the time to do this. This is why shops – and my doctor's practice – shut the doors when they know they will not be at their busiest and then they get on with the business of training. Having allocated the required time, you will also need to be well organized. As the trainer, you must set clear objectives (yes, you

SELF-ASSESSMENT

COULD YOU RUN A TRAINING EVENT?

If you are to act as training manager for your organization, then you will need a variety of skills and attributes. This questionnaire is designed to help you to decide if you have these and can apply them to designing, organizing and delivering a training event. Answer the questions as honestly as you can and consider each attribute carefully:

1. Are you organized? Do you have experience of managing an event and preparing reports, etc.?
2. Can you manage your time – and your other commitments – to ensure that you have sufficient free time to spend on the additional major project that a training event represents?
3. How much time can you find to spend on the necessary research and the design and development of course material?
4. How much time can you spare away from your normal workplace, and in one block, for the delivery of the training event?
5. Do you have the confidence and composure to stand in front of the delegates and deliver presentations?
6. Do you have the interpersonal skills necessary to manage a group of delegates and to involve them in your training event?
7. Can you set goals – and meet them? Do you fully understand where your organization is going and how it is going to get there?
8. Are you prepared to spend time after the course evaluating its success – or otherwise?
9. Do you need training to become a competent trainer? If so, are you prepared to undertake the necessary training?
10. Do you have sufficient understanding of the subject matter of the planned training event?

figure 1 self-assessment questionnaire

must have objectives to keep you on track – even for a short event), have a tight running order and also the discipline to start on time. An even bigger discipline is to finish on time, so that the staff can be sent back to their work without delay. Remember, if you do not keep to this last point, the training will not prove popular with the delegates' line managers – no matter what their people have learned.

Summary

- Setting SMART objectives for every training event is vital.
- Try to calculate the worth of the benefits obtained from the course so that you will be able to compare it with the total costs to assess cost-effectiveness.
- If you decide to use an external provider, do your research carefully to avoid an expensive mistake.
- If you are considering designing and running your own course, assess your aptitudes using the form provided to help you decide, then start small – perhaps with a regular short shot of training.

Revision test

1. Learning objectives must be 'SMART'. What does this mean?
2. Name three types of direct costs of a training course.
3. What altruistic benefit might an organization gain as a result of training its staff?
4. For what sort of delegates should you not choose a course based on listening and then completing written exercises?
5. What should you do if you are considering a course from an external provider with whom you are unfamiliar?
6. What is usually the main limiting factor when choosing between internal and external courses?
7. What is 'generic content' in terms of an external training course?
8. Name three sources of information about the training market.
9. What is the main requirement for ensuring that short, in-house training sessions are run regularly?
10. How can you assess your own potential for becoming an internal training provider?

05 becoming a trainer – preparation

In this chapter you will:

- **find out what preparation is necessary before developing an effective course or seminar**
- **get tips on how to produce notes and written materials for your course**

Preparation

When you have conducted your training needs analysis, found that some training is needed and have decided that you will design and deliver at least part of this requirement yourself, what do you do next? With confidence, organization and preparation, becoming a trainer is 'do-able'. However, before you begin to design your training event (more on design in the next chapter), there are a few things to consider. You must develop a training strategy. During your training needs analysis you may have identified a broad requirement for training within your organization. You should also have delved further and identified individual training needs. Following this, you then need to consider exactly what type of training will fulfil those individual needs while delivering the benefits that your organization needs. You are likely to find that you will need to employ a variety of different options such as:

- a training course or seminar
- on-the-job training
- coaching
- mentoring
- distance learning
- brainstorming/discussion groups

Alongside this, you must know – or get to know – your trainees and your venue. You must also know exactly what you are aiming at and be very clear as to how you are going to get to where you want to be. If you are able to focus on the outcome at this stage, then you are much more likely to achieve it, so write down your desired outcome and keep it in front of you all the time you are working on your course design or training strategy.

If you decide that an internal course will suit your purpose, whether you are preparing to design a course for your own team or a course for someone else in your organization, you should gather together the following information:

- exactly what the training need is
- who will be receiving the training
- the learning objective
- the approximate duration – taking into account your budget, the knowledge and skills to be imparted and the needs of the business
- a working title for the event
- how much time and money can be spent on this project

How important is preparation?

The best way to illustrate just how important preparation is to the success of a training event is to consider what can go wrong if a trainer is inadequately prepared. An unsuccessful training event will probably follow if more than just one or two of these elements of inferior preparation are present:

- the wrong environment – too big or too small, incorrect layout
- a lack of planning – housekeeping matters such as accommodation and catering can make a big difference to any event
- a lack of clear training objectives
- inferior visual aids – this can refer to the quality of the visual aids or to the quantity or appropriateness of them
- boring delivery – remember to include variety in your course and tailor it to your delegates
- a stilted delivery – speech is different from written language, and things that would appear OK if read in a newspaper or in an academic book will not necessarily sound right when said out loud; make sure that any presentation is written so that it can be delivered verbally
- poor quality notes that do not get used after the event
- course content that is too wide-ranging – the course content must be closely linked to your training objectives; if something doesn't add to the chance of your objectives being met, leave it out!

Next, we'll look at what you need to know, or find out, about the prospective delegates.

Know your audience

The importance of knowing your audience will become clear when you consider two distinct groups:

1 Delegates who are used to applying practical skills – such as machine operatives, assembly workers, and craft workers – may not respond well to a request to learn solely from written materials.
2 Senior management delegates will not appreciate materials written at a very basic level.

As you can see from these two examples, the skills and aptitudes of the delegates to whom you are presenting will dictate the type of material that you prepare. Different types of people will have different preferred ways to receive and to communicate information. Your whole course or seminar should be carefully targeted for your audience – so get to know them.

Apart from the example of practical versus academic skills, you should also consider:

- age range – review your materials and remove references that do not cater for the age range of your audience; this might include allusions to music performers who were popular before most of your delegates were born or, maybe just as bad, mention of current musicians to an audience of over-fifties – plan your examples, case studies and illustrations with care
- gender – men and women may have different learning styles and different understanding of some issues
- ethnicity and religion – take care not to offend
- educational level – pitch your material at the right level for your group
- current concerns of the delegates – take care that you are aware of problems (such as redundancy situations) that may cause them to be critical of the company
- whether they are here voluntarily – it may be harder work to present to an audience who have been ordered to attend compared with a well-motivated audience who are attending by choice

As you can see, there are a great many issues that need to be taken into account so that the material is right for your audience. You should also try to understand their motivation. In almost everything we do there will be an element of 'what's in it for me?', so make an attempt to figure out their drivers (motivating factors) when you are planning your material. Their drivers may include financial rewards, job satisfaction, a sense of achievement, personal development, recognition, job security or simply curiosity. Try to tap into these motivating factors as you go through your material. Let's look at how you might build motivation into your course plans to satisfy some of these factors:

1. Achievement – people like to achieve so perhaps including a test and then a certificate at the end of the course stating that the individual delegate has 'successfully completed the course' will satisfy this need.
2. Promotion or job satisfaction – if people are looking for promotion or to do more interesting work (or to do their existing work to a higher standard), then the possibility of the

things they are going to learn helping them in this aim should be mentioned during the course. Perhaps you could make reference to this in your learning objectives for the training event and give examples of where the knowledge can be put to appropriate use.

3 Recognition – your feedback during the course can go some way towards fulfilling this need so make sure that you plan for these vital sessions. The certificate mentioned above will also be valued.
4 Curiosity – some people have an inbuilt desire to learn so merely presenting new information to them will satisfy this. People seeking personal development will also have their needs met by being given extra knowledge and skills so build reference to this into your initial sessions. Showing them how to improve their performance by using the newly acquired knowledge will help to bring the benefits required by the organization.

Of course, there will also be delegates for whom there is no motivating factor. They are attending your training event because they do not have a choice. They may even consider that they do not need any training in the area that you are presenting. This type of delegate should have been discovered during your appraisals and training needs analysis and you will need to carefully explain your objectives. It can be very satisfying if you can win them round.

To sum up, you must do the research necessary to ensure that you know your audience. Find out as much as possible about them including who they are (age, gender, educational level, current job), what they already know (level at which they are currently working, qualifications, courses previously attended) and what they need and want (motivations, their managers' requirements and expectations of the course, learning objectives – what they want to learn and why). If you do not know who your audience is, you will not be in a position to produce an appropriate training session. To be effective, training must be tailored to meet the needs of your audience.

Know your environment

When you are presenting a training course or seminar, your surroundings are very important. The 'feel' of the room can affect your performance – for good or bad. Get to know the room that you will be using and consider how its size, shape and acoustics will affect your presentation – will it be a large room, filled with delegates or perhaps with only a few delegates huddled in a corner, or will it be a very small room with a few people comfortably ensconced or too many people for the space available?

Consider how many delegates will be in the space available and how they will be seated around the room – this could affect your choice of visual aid. A flipchart will not be of much use to you during a presentation in a large hall with a hundred delegates, nor will a presentation featuring hundreds of slides be appropriate for a training event for just two or three of your colleagues.

Apart from the main room – for the delivery of the majority of your training sessions – you may also need to have one or more anterooms available. Depending on the content of your training event, small rooms away from the main room could be needed for use during syndicate exercises, for example, or for private interviews, group work and discussions. If you are planning several group discussions or syndicate exercises, then a venue with just one large room available may not be suitable. It might be possible to create different spaces, however, with the use of portable screens or with the arrangement of the furniture. Don't forget to check that the anterooms are open and suitably equipped – it is not unknown for perfect rooms to be unavailable because they are locked! The important thing is to plan the use of the venue in advance of your training event.

The way you lay out your training room will have an effect on the way training sessions are delivered. There are a number of different layouts and, if possible, you should choose the one that suits your personal style and the type of course you are planning. These layouts include:

- **Around a large central table.** This is similar to a boardroom with everyone seated around a large table or cluster of tables with the trainer at the top of the table. This is a useful layout for internal courses as it will be the one most commonly found in the room that many organizations have to use. It can help with team building and also helps the trainer to be viewed as part of the team. The main drawback to this layout is that some people – say at the corners of the table – may not get a good view of any visual aids used at the front of the room.

- **All facing the front.** This is the classroom layout where all tables/desks are in rows facing the front. It can be useful for formal teaching situations and also, given sufficient space, the desks may be rearranged when syndicate exercises are carried out. The disadvantages of this layout are that it does not foster a team spirit and the trainees at the back may get a poor view.
- **Around a U-shape.** Here the tables are placed together in two rows facing one another with a gap up the middle and more tables linking the tables across one end. This might not be practical for many companies as it does require a lot of space, but if you can set up your room like this it offers the advantage of the trainer being able to walk up the middle amongst the delegates and, as they can all see one another, it can help to make the atmosphere informal and less intimidating than the other layouts.

A further point to watch when assessing external venues is that delegates may have to travel long distances. You should take this into account when planning your sessions – can all the delegates get there in time for the opening session? Do you need to close the session at a specific time? You should attempt to control as much as possible about your training event. The venue and the actual room (or rooms) used will play a very important part in determining the style and effectiveness of your presentation.

Creating notes that work

TRAINING TIP

Before creating notes, ask yourself what you want the delegates to have learned at the end of the session and build your notes around this.

Handouts should only be for use after the training session. If you hand out notes before or during the session then you will find that you will lose the attention of some, if not all, of your delegates. You should, however, announce at the start of the session that notes will be available later so that trainees do not have to make their own notes. Most trainees appreciate the effort that goes into producing good quality handouts.

Good quality notes must:

- not be so short as to miss important points or so complex that they are difficult to understand
- not be so long as to deter delegates from bothering to read them
- be specific to the course; always create new notes for each course that you run – do not be tempted to re-use old notes
- keep to the same running order as the training session – if the structure was good enough for the course, then it will be good enough for the notes
- contain a summary of the key points at the end of each section
- contain plenty of sub-headings and bullet-pointed lists as these break down large chunks of material and make it easier to remember

When compiling your handouts, consider including a few self-assessment questions in them. If you put these after the summary of each section and leave space for the delegates to write in their answers, they will be able to check their own progress.

Don't forget the possibility of including ready-made documents with your own handouts. Examples of appropriate items to use in this way include manufacturers' instruction booklets (following a course on the use of a new machine), company brochures and newsletters (after an induction course), and government or professional bodies' leaflets (after a Health and Safety event). It should go without saying that any handouts should be good quality copies. If you are able to present them in a smart folder or binder, then the perceived value of your notes will rise and the chance of them getting used after the course will be increased.

Summary

- When deciding on the type of training to suit each training need, you should keep the required outcome in mind.
- Get to know your delegates so that you can tailor the training to their needs, aptitudes and motivations.
- The training venue can affect your presentation so get to know it and give careful consideration to the best layout for your style of presentation.
- Produce concise, good quality notes that will be used after the course.

Revision test

1 Name three things that you should consider when tailoring a course to your delegates.
2 Which two motivating factors or drivers would be satisfied by the issuing of a certificate for a course?
3 What might you need extra rooms for, in addition to the main training room, during a training event?
4 Describe a 'classroom layout' for a training session.
5 What order should you use for handouts for a training course?
6 Give three examples of ready-made documents that could be used in addition to your own handouts?
7 When should you give out handouts?
8 Why is a layout based around a large central table useful for internal courses in particular?
9 What two actions can a trainer take to ensure that his or her delivery is not boring?
10 What question should you ask yourself when starting to create notes for a training event?

06 designing a course

In this chapter you will:

- **learn how to decide on the content of your course so that it is both interesting and effective**
- **review your presentation skills**

A balanced structure

The first thing to remember when putting a course or seminar together is that the course has an objective. Write it down and keep it in front of you. This might be a good time to expand your objectives in light of the course that you are now planning. Ask yourself a few questions such as:

- What do I want the delegates to know, or feel or to be able to do at the end of the training?
- How will their working routines be changed by what I have to tell them?
- Who needs to be satisfied with what the course achieves? (you, the delegates, the delegates' bosses, your boss, the company's financial people, the Human Resources Department?)

Your aim must be to ensure that at the completion of the training the delegates have learned what they are supposed to have learned. To this end, a simple but effective approach is:

- tell them what you are going to tell them
- tell them
- tell them what you've told them

This repetition means that you must find a variety of ways to get the important information across. There are two reasons for this. Firstly, people have different learning styles (more of this in Chapter 8) so, for example, one person may find written information easy to understand and remember, whereas another person may find it easier to retain information that has had some practical element such as role-play or a discussion exercise. Secondly, you should avoid boredom at all costs. Delegates who find their attention wandering or, worse still, who fall asleep will not achieve your objectives so vary the type of content from session to session. Intersperse a presentation with a syndicate exercise, or add in a short video alongside a guided discussion of the principles explained in the video, for example. If a course consists solely of someone standing at the front of the room presenting slides and talking a lot, then the delegates are likely to get bored and the outcome will not be a successful one.

Now is a good time to come up with a good title for your training event. It needs to sum up the content and aim of the training, of course, but it should also, if you can manage it, arouse interest. A course aimed at improving how your organization deals with customer complaints, for example, could be entitled 'Customer Service Procedures'. This might encapsulate perfectly what the course is about but it will not get much interest, nor will it get your delegates raring to go. You may add in the word 'new' as this is always more interesting than the same old methods. You could also lengthen the title by adding something that answers your delegates' question of 'what's in it for me?' So, in this case, you could try the title 'The new Customer Service Procedures – how to make your customers happy and easier to deal with'. A good title will go a small part of the way towards achieving your goal by getting the delegates' interest from the start, so give this aspect of your course some thought.

Keeping your objectives, as well as the need for variety, in mind you have to decide on the content of the course and also the order in which you will present it. The temptation is to try to write a scintillating introduction then go on to develop the main body of the course and so on in chronological order. However, this is the wrong approach, as the opener should introduce the course to the delegates (tell them what you're going to tell them) and this is impossible to do effectively until you have written the bulk of the materials. It is vital to develop your main sessions first.

The body of the course

Make sure that the sessions that make up the main part of your event give you a logical progression towards your objectives. Try to vary the pace by including a number of the following:

- listening sessions
- syndicate exercises
- role-plays
- visual aids
- question-and-answer sessions
- case studies to discuss
- written exercises
- tests

TRAINING TIP

Get organized! Put the main topics on index cards and add ideas for illustrations, case studies, etc. to each one as you think of them. You can then move the cards around until you come to a satisfactory order for the training event.

In developing your main sessions you should first collate the information you already have to hand and divide it into appropriate topics – perhaps in folders or on index cards – then decide what further research is necessary. You could conduct a brainstorming session – either alone or with colleagues – to help. This is where you will get all your ideas together and the sessions will begin to take shape. You may come up with anecdotes, graphs, ideas for slides or videos, case studies and exercises. Write down all the thoughts and ideas you have at this stage or you may forget them later. If, as is likely, you need more material there are lots of resources available to you:

- the internet
- libraries
- colleagues
- articles
- books
- notes from other courses

When you have all the material you need and have separated it into the various topic headings you will be able to put them into a workable sequence. This is easier if you have used index cards as they can be moved around until you are happy that you have the correct sequence.

The introduction

Only after you have built the main body of your course or seminar can you add the introduction. As we all know, 'first impressions count' so this is a very important step, especially for a new trainer. Your aim should be to grab the attention of all the delegates – and keep it!

It is at this point that you will set the tone of the session (more about the presentation skills for this in Chapter 7). It is important that you cover the following three issues in the introductory session:

1 Ensure that the delegates are aware of the event's learning objectives. As discussed earlier, your objectives for the training event should be carefully composed and should be written down. It is a good idea to display the objective right at the start of the event – perhaps on a slide or flipchart. You can then display it again at the start of each session to keep the objective in the delegates' minds (and yours).
2 Advise them of your expectations as to their behaviour and participation during the training. Setting a few ground rules

at the start of the event can pay dividends later. Depending upon the age and usual standards of behaviour of the delegates, you may have to emphasize the importance of good timekeeping and let them know that being negative towards their fellow delegates is not acceptable. Give them a schedule for the sessions, including lunch and refreshment breaks, and let them know that you expect them to keep to it so that you can all meet the event's objectives.

Another issue that you need to discuss here is that of asking questions. When do you want the delegates to ask questions? Unless you are very confident that questions scattered throughout your presentation will not put you off your stride, you would be well advised to ask the delegates to save their questions for the end of each session.

Use this part of the session to impress upon the delegates the importance of their participation and co-operation for their own benefit and that of the other delegates. Try to enthuse them about what they are going to learn together and to instil a little team spirit at this point. After all, for the duration of the course the delegates will form a team – with you as their temporary leader – and if you can all work together, the success of the training event will be more likely.

3 Plan some time into this introductory session for a few 'housekeeping' matters such as:

- emergency arrangements (fire drills, medical problems, etc.)
- catering – where and when will lunch and any refreshments be served
- timings
- introducing yourself, plus any guest speakers and presenters, and getting the delegates to do the same
- toilet locations
- smoking policy
- venue facilities such as car parking and relaxation areas
- accommodation facilities, if appropriate (sports facilities, for example)
- switch off mobile phones
- expenses arrangements – if delegates are staying overnight, what they are expected to pay for and what the company will pay for
- any questions – make sure everyone is comfortable, and remember, if there is something else taking their attention, they will not be concentrating on the training

Plan your opening words carefully. They should, as we have said, gain the attention of your delegates right from the start. Perhaps you can start with an interesting statistic connected with the main subject matter of your course (for example, 'nine out of ten customers who are dissatisfied will just take their business away' for a customer services course) or a relevant quotation, anecdote or story. Whatever you choose, it should be short and its relevance easily understood.

The closing session

Your next step is to summarize the material for your closing session (tell them what you've told them). A short quiz or discussion may be helpful at this stage to check what the delegates have learned, to reinforce your previous sessions and to draw the whole course together. This is also your chance to make a good last impression. It is not the time to raise new issues, so avoid the temptation to bring in some new information. Simply sum up what you want the delegates to take away from the session and thank them for attending. Try to make it a strong ending rather than letting the event peter out weakly.

You will also need to conduct an event evaluation during this closing session (more of this in Chapter 10).

Linking the sessions

Finally, you will need to add some links between all the sessions so that the whole thing hangs together and flows smoothly. These are like signposts. They point the way to the next session, so you may say something along the lines of, 'Our next session, after lunch, will develop this point and show you how you can put some of what you have learned into action' or, 'What questions do you have on this topic? After we've discussed those we'll have a short break before we go on to a syndicate exercise on what we've learned.' Again, it is important to keep your objective in mind and to keep referring back to it.

Planning forms

It is a good idea to develop a document for each session to help with planning. You can use these to record:

- the planned duration of each session plus the start and finish times

- the learning objective for each session
- housekeeping details such as which room is to be used, room layout and so on
- what materials you will need – notes, visual aids, etc.
- what equipment will be needed
- notes on what you should emphasize from the subject areas

These planning forms will help you to stay organized and to remember all the things that you may forget in the last-minute flurry of activity when you are running a training event.

Content

The content of your training event will obviously be tailored very closely to your organization's needs but, as stated previously, you should aim at a course or seminar that will keep the interest of your delegates and also ensure that they learn what you want them to learn. For these reasons you should vary your presenting methods. In addition to the usual listening sessions plus the use of visual aids (more details of these in Chapter 8), quizzes and tests, the pace and content can be varied by the inclusion of different exercises that will involve the delegates. These participation exercises include role-plays and syndicate work.

Role-play

Role-play involving case studies allows delegates to practise the skills and knowledge that they have learned, in a safe environment. It is a useful way for you to evaluate the level to which they have understood the course content and to which they will be able to put the learning into practice when they return to their workplace. To set up a role-play session you will need to devise a situation that the groups of delegates can use. This could be a real-life situation or one that you have conjured up out of your imagination. Whichever you choose it must, of course, relate to the topic being studied. So, for example, for a course on negotiating you might present the delegates with notes on real-life situations, such as negotiating with a customer in a sales situation or haggling for goods in a market. To be effective learning exercises, role-play situations must be managed carefully:

- split the delegates into pairs

- present them with written briefs on a situation
- give each delegate the chance to play both of the parts in the role-play
- advise them that their actions must be as close to real life as possible and that this is role-play not an acting audition!
- allow time for both delegates to read the notes and to consider their strategy prior to starting the role-play – perhaps 10 minutes
- give a time limit for the actual role-playing – maybe 10 or 15 minutes – then switch the roles and continue for a further 10 or 15 minutes
- observe the role-plays, then spend some time giving the delegates feedback on their performances and getting feedback from them

The participants will derive some benefit from considering their responses and those of their partners in the role-plays and then further learning can take place during the feedback following the session. You will all get maximum learning from the role-plays if the feedback is carefully handled. Make sure that you start with getting the participants' reactions as to how they thought they handled the situation, then draw out the ways in which the knowledge they have gained from the training was used – or not used! – in the role-play.

Syndicate exercises

These are similar to role-play exercises in that the delegates have to work together to discuss and solve problems. Syndicate exercises usually involve more delegates – perhaps four or more depending upon the total number of delegates – so that they have to work as a team. This type of exercise can deliver valuable benefits such as team-building and problem-solving skills in addition to the feedback opportunities provided. When the delegates are called upon to deliver the results of the exercises, you will be able to see whether they have become competent at using their newly acquired knowledge in simulated business situations.

When you are planning a syndicate exercise as part of a training event, you will need to devise situations, presented like a story with plenty of information to accompany them, that the groups of delegates can discuss, and work on, to come up with a solution to the problem that the situation poses. An example of this type of case study could be a warehouse or other factory department that needs reorganizing. The notes for the exercise should then include, for example, data on the quantities and sizes of the products to be stored, the throughput of the department, number of staff and costs involved. Problems should be described such as those involving staffing levels (high costs or shortages for example) and space requirements (whether a new warehouse is rented to deal with seasonal overspills, for instance). The syndicate dealing with this case study would then be required to retire to the syndicate room (or any quiet area that can be organized for each group), to discuss the problem and analyse the data provided. They then have to come up with their recommendations as to the solution to the problem posed. These recommendations can be presented to the group in the form of a written report. Alternatively, they could also be presented verbally, thereby using the opportunities for further learning when the delegates have to develop and deliver a presentation. The other delegates can give feedback on the syndicate's conclusions and reasoning.

Syndicate exercises are an important learning tool as they involve the practice of the following processes:

- group debate
- questioning
- assimilating quantities of data
- prioritization
- problem-solving
- reporting back
- presentational skills

Continuing the theme of using this type of exercise as an opportunity to give and receive feedback, syndicates can be set up to learn how to deliver – and accept – criticism. This needs to be carefully set up, of course, to ensure that the delegates are not de-motivated nor upset by criticism and that personality clashes are not allowed to inform the criticism. To this end, choose the groups carefully, making sure that a blend of characters are in each group and that you do not put together any two delegates who you may have noticed are antagonistic towards each other. Brief the teams, emphasizing that the criticism will be both given and received by each person in turn, and that the aim of the exercise is to learn how to deal with this process. In addition you will have to set limits on the number of criticisms – perhaps three positive points and three areas for improvement. State quite clearly that there are to be no personal attacks – any negative points must be made so that the delegates are given the chance to improve their performance in a business setting. Give them some examples of the sorts of attributes – and failings – that you are looking to highlight, for instance, 'good at working in a team', 'highly organized', 'does not meet deadlines', 'goes into too much detail' or 'needs to believe in his own abilities'. Each person must take a turn to leave the room while the remaining delegates in their group have a short discussion (perhaps 10 or 15 minutes) to decide which points they will give to their absent colleague. When the person returns they could be given a flipchart and marker and then will have to write up the points – negative and positive – that are made. This gives the person receiving the criticism something to do while they are being criticized as it can be a very uncomfortable experience to sit looking at colleagues during this time. The trainer's job during these exercises will be to 'keep the peace', smoothing over any areas of disagreement and keeping the session going. At the same time it will be possible to evaluate how the delegates are responding and how they are using the lessons learned.

For all types of syndicate exercises, you must have a debriefing session to make sure that no unresolved issues were uncovered and that the delegates are taking the right lessons away with them. Ask them how the delegates felt the session went and what they learned from it. As always, try to make sure that all delegates contribute to such sessions.

The importance of timing

Successful training events are run by people who know where they are going, how they are going to get there – and when! Having decided upon the training objectives and the course content, you must then make sure that the course can be accomplished in the time allowed. Overrun and you will be in danger of irritating your delegates by keeping them away from either their jobs or their private lives. In this case you may lose the attention of your delegates and may not achieve your learning objectives. However, if you finish too early you will be left with an embarrassing gap at the end of your session (although just a few minutes will be acceptable and probably hardly noticed) and it will be very hard to get rid of the impression of incompetence that this will create in your delegates' minds about you. Delivering subsequent training sessions will be made much more difficult as a result of this.

Don't forget to leave sufficient time for questions at the end of each session.

You will also want to be sure, when planning your event, that the correct amount of time is devoted to each of the topics that you are intending to cover. For this you will need to do a number of things:

- Prioritize – you will not want to allocate more time to a simple session on a topic that is well within your delegates' capabilities than to a more complicated session dealing with hard-to-understand subjects.
- Advise guest speakers of the amount of time that you have allotted and obtain their commitment to keeping to time.
- Allow a set amount of time for syndicate exercises – these will take a minimum of 20 minutes but may take up to a whole day. Whatever you decide, make sure that the time allocated can be justified in terms of the exercise's contribution to the learning objectives.
- Do a dummy run. If this is a new training session (one that has not been used previously), you will need to estimate the time it will take to get through the presentation. Do this by reading through the prepared material at the appropriate speed. Don't forget to allow time for the delegates to settle down and for a short introduction to the session (including stating that all-important objective). You will also need a round-up with time for questions, evaluation and comments at the end.
- Allow time for 'housekeeping' – advising delegates about the arrangements that have been made for meals, accommodation, health and safety matters, etc.
- Plan in some time for lunch, refreshments and 'comfort breaks'.
- Decide upon a maximum time for each session length – 90 minutes is usually accepted as the longest time that you should expect delegates to sit and listen. Any longer than this will mean that they begin to get restless and this may well interrupt your concentration.

In addition to the amount of time you allow for each session, you will also need to think about the running order. This must be logical in terms of working towards the learning objective. Think of the individual training sessions as building blocks. They must slot together in just the right order, with the base blocks – the sessions containing elementary pieces of information – coming early in the training event, and the final pieces being delivered when your delegates have assimilated all the initial information and are ready for the finer detail.

When you are delivering a training session always keep time in mind. Keep a careful check on how your sessions are running compared with your timed plans. Do not, however, constantly (or even occasionally) consult your wristwatch. Your delegates will notice this and it may have an unsettling effect. They may start checking the time themselves, wondering how long to the next break, or they may jump to the conclusion that the presenter is bored – and that can be infectious! Instead, try to position yourself so that you have a clear view of a clock in the room or, if a clock is not available, take off your wristwatch and place it by your materials so that you can check how time is progressing without attracting your delegates' attention.

What presentation skills do you need?

Being a trainer is a specialized position that requires expertise in the skills necessary not only to design and plan training courses but also to deliver the training and handle the feedback and evaluation to complete the process of training successfully. If the trainer is inadequately skilled then the learning objectives will be more difficult to meet.

If the trainer in your organization is to be you and you have not previously had experience of, or training in, course development and delivery, then you should ensure that you set aside time for yourself to learn the necessary skills as your first priority.

The presentation skills you need include:

- being able to set training aims and objectives
- being able to build the structure of training sessions
- techniques of presentation – projection of your voice, stance, etc.
- using visual aids
- handling different learning types
- handling questions
- evaluating training sessions
- being able to ensure that learning is used back in the workplace

All of these skills can be learned. With confidence, determination – and, of course, utilizing the tips in this book – you should be able to take on training responsibilities.

If you are new to presenting a training session, start modestly. Organize a short session on a topic in which you are confident and practise your delivery until you are comfortable with your performance. Familiarity with the materials and keeping your objective at the front of your mind will ensure success.

TOP TIPS FOR DELIVERY

- Get to know your materials.
- Get to know your equipment.
- Keep your audience in mind.
- Make eye contact.
- Don't fidget or mumble.
- Remember that your delegates are your customers.
- Always be working towards your learning goals.

Creating a good learning environment

What is a good learning environment? Is it just a comfortable room that all the delegates will fit into? For a training event to be successful there is far more to selecting the right venue and creating an environment conducive to learning than merely finding a big enough room with heating!

Your choice of a training room may well be limited by your budget or by what is available in-house. If you do have a reasonable amount of say, however, there are a number of things to bear in mind when choosing a suitable venue and these vary according to whether the facilities are in-house or external.

In-house facilities

Training facilities within an organization could be either solely for training purposes (specially designed perhaps with all the audio-visual aids that you could wish for) or, more likely, rooms that can be used for training purposes after they have been converted from their regular use. This latter might include the company boardroom, spare offices, the canteen or offices for use outside normal working hours.

If you are lucky enough to work in an organization that has rooms specially designated for training, then the choice is made for you. The costs will be minimal as the facilities are already in place and you will not need to worry about equipment for visual aids, travel arrangements, catering or overnight accommodation. This is the ideal situation, although problems might be encountered if strict discipline about restricting interruptions is not maintained or if you are competing with other parts of the organization for access to the facilities.

Most small organizations do not have specially designed training facilities but may be able to muster a suitable room that can be used temporarily for any training event. Again you will not have problems regarding travelling, catering and accommodation, but you will still have to ensure that your delegates give the training their full attention and do not behave as if they were still at work. For this, you will have to enlist the support of the delegates' managers and colleagues to ensure that there are no interruptions. It can be useful to advise them of the break times and ask them to restrict any contact with delegates to those times. And put a 'Do Not Disturb' notice on the training room door!

It is worthwhile making sure that the room is properly equipped and that the layout is as you require, as otherwise the training event could be marred by a feeling that it is not important enough to spend any money and that it is somehow not 'real training'.

External facilities

Training facilities outside the organization may be hotel conference rooms or other local venues that may be suitable for your event. Hotel facilities are usually specially designed and equipped for training events of various sizes and duration. Here you will be free of interruptions and the delegates should be able to concentrate on the training as they will be away from their place of work. There will also be the advantage of having catering facilities and overnight accommodation readily available. A further advantage of this type of venue is that, in staying overnight, you can not only extend the time available for training sessions but also will probably be able to keep the delegates together in the evenings to ensure that a bit of team-building and bonding goes on. The downside of this convenience is, of course, that hiring these facilities can be very expensive and that choosing such a venue – and getting it right – is that bit more difficult.

Venues other than hotel facilities might be less expensive and may serve your purpose in getting the delegates away from work. Some local knowledge of what is available will help you here so ask around within your organization and also friends and family who might know suitable function rooms available locally. This could include schools and colleges, local authority facilities, village halls, museums, art galleries – almost anywhere that people gather, so use your imagination. If you opt for one of these alternative venues you will need to ensure that everyone can travel easily every day to the venue – or that accommodation is available – and that you arrange your own equipment for the presentation. Make sure that you visit the venue and give yourself enough time to set the room up as you want it.

Whatever the arrangements you make for your training event, you should do everything possible to ensure that you have a comfortable, well-lit room with sufficient space and equipment to carry out all the different types of session that you have planned. Make sure that the catering available is suitable. And remember, your delegates will learn much more easily if they are in comfortable surroundings, so getting the venue right is important to your training objectives.

Summary

- Aim at a balance of different types of learning experience to avoid boring the delegates.
- Reinforce your learning objectives by using a beginning, a middle and an end as the basic structure for your presentation (tell them what you're going to tell them, tell them, and tell them what you've told them).
- Use as many sources as necessary when you are researching your course content.
- Try to include exercises that will ensure that delegates participate in the training sessions rather than just sit and listen.
- Get organized – use index cards or files to keep all your ideas together.
- Pay particular attention to the timing of your sessions and practice to ensure that your session can be run to time.
- If you're going to deliver a training event, make sure that you allow sufficient time for training yourself.
- Choose a venue where the delegates can be comfortable and where you can minimize disruptions.

Revision test

1 What should you do with your training objective when you are planning a training event?
2 What are you aiming at when you are devising a title for your course?
3 Describe one way that you can devise a running order for your training event.
4 What should you plan first for a training event – the introduction, the main body or the closing session?
5 Name three ways that you could open a training session.
6 Name three things that you should include on your planning forms.
7 How long might a role-play exercise last?
8 What do you need to leave time for at the end of each training session?
9 Name three types of room that could be used for an in-house training event.
10 Name three venues, apart from hotel conference facilities, where you could hold a training event outside your organization's premises.

07 delivery

In this chapter you will:

- **look at the differences between a good presentation and a bad one**
- **learn how to keep the training session going with discussions and activities**

That all-important first impression

Most people will feel anxious just before starting any sort of presentation. Whether experienced or inexperienced, someone delivering an internal course will be no exception to this. It is universally accepted that a good first impression really counts, and this can add to the stress felt by the presenter as he or she stands up in front of a number of delegates to start the first training session. You need to appear confident and competent – even though you might not feel either of these things – and this impression can be planned. Here are some tips on starting a training session:

- Greet everyone as they enter the training venue. Don't be tempted to enter the room when everyone has arrived – then you will not be controlling the impression that the delegates form when they are in the room waiting for you. Be there first and meet your delegates with a smile. Don't try to avoid eye contact by busying yourself making last-minute adjustments to your materials – eye contact is essential right from the start of your presentation as it gives an impression of confidence, credibility and competence.
- Start on time. You may have to cope with the one or two people who turn up late but this is preferable to wasting time and letting your carefully planned timetable be jeopardized. It also sends out an important message – that you value their time and yours.
- Declare your objectives for the course – if you're using slides, then prepare one stating your objectives and display it so that everyone knows what you – and they – are aiming at. Alternatively, write them up on a flipchart or make it your first slide in a PowerPoint presentation.
- Don't sit down. If you're standing up you will appear more confident, you will find that you will breathe more easily and will be able to project your voice so that everyone can hear you. In addition it gives you a position of authority and influence.
- Speak up, don't mumble. Check the faces of the people sitting furthest away from you. If they're paying attention and not betraying signs of boredom or puzzlement, then everyone can hear you. There's no need to ask!
- Try not to betray your nervousness with little, annoying habits – jingling your change in your pocket, for example, or tapping your pencil on the desk in front of you. Keep your fingers away from your face too – if your mouth is obscured

by your hands, some may find it difficult to tell what you are saying.

- Be prepared. Nothing will make you feel easier about the forthcoming session than knowing that everything that can be done to make it go smoothly has been done.
- Devise a good opening gambit for yourself and practise it again and again. Familiarity will give you confidence

What is a good presentation?

A good presentation will have three vital characteristics:

1 A presenter – or trainer – who is comfortable and able to be himself.

2 A presenter who knows and understands his audience. As we've discussed previously, there are two main reasons for this requirement. Firstly, it will not be possible either to plan the necessary materials or to deliver the course at the right level if you are not fully aware of your delegates' aptitudes. Secondly, it is vital that you understand the delegates' motivations. Are they there because they do not have a choice or because they want to be? Do they really want to improve their performance and do they understand how the training will help them to do this? The answers to these questions will help you to deliver a good presentation that holds the attention of the delegates and gets your message across effectively.

3 Preparation. Although it is natural to be nervous, a thorough knowledge of the subject and familiarity with your course materials will make you feel more at ease. Do not try to be perfect, but aim at competence and keep your objectives in mind. The value of preparation, including practising your delivery, cannot be overstated.

Your aim as presenter is to appear confident and well prepared and to deliver a training event that will fulfil your learning objectives. You are also aiming to do all this while keeping the delegates interested and making the best possible use of their time.

By contrast a poor presentation may be badly planned so that the delegates are left hanging around while the trainer gathers his materials or they will be resentful at the overrun that will happen if the timing is not carefully planned. Upsetting the delegates in this way is not to be recommended, as irritated delegates will not learn well. Most delegates will quickly spot a serious lack of preparation and once you have lost their respect it will be very difficult to win it back and your job will not be an easy one.

Above all, a bad presentation will be one that does not have well-defined learning objectives that are clearly conveyed to the delegates from the very start of the training event.

TOP TEN TIPS FOR PRESENTERS

1. Look them in the eye. Make eye contact with each and every delegate. If you avoid this you will appear shifty and unconvincing.
2. Don't read from notes. Use brief prompts – perhaps on cards – that you have prepared in advance to keep you on track.
3. Do use visual aids to illustrate the points you are making.
4. Don't patronize the delegates. If you use jargon that they may not be familiar with or try to make everything appear too complicated, they will not be impressed and they won't learn much either!
5. Don't fidget. Be aware of all the annoying little habits that may make an appearance when you are nervous – jingling change in pockets, rubbing your face, swaying from side-to-side, etc.
6. Don't look inefficient – make a list of items you need for each session, for example OHP, spare bulbs, screen, number of slides, handouts, pens, notes, prompt cards, etc.
7. Don't talk too much about yourself. The delegates are there to learn about the subject of the training event – not your life story.
8. Try to sound convincing. If you don't sound as though you believe what you're saying, why should the delegates?
9. Avoid making jokes unless you're an accomplished, confident comedian.
10. Practise, practise, practise.

How to keep the session alive

Everyone can appreciate that you must keep the interest of your delegates if you are going to achieve your learning objectives. Here are three signs that attention is wandering and the trainees are flagging:

1 trainees yawning
2 trainees looking out of the window
3 trainees leaning backwards in their seats

Three signs that they are still listening are:

1 their attention is focused on the speaker and their facial expressions indicate interest
2 they're leaning forward – a sign of alertness and interest
3 they're nodding to indicate understanding and agreement

So what can you do to keep their interest? There will no doubt be occasions during your presentation when you will feel that you are 'losing' your trainees. If you're facing a sea of bored faces, don't just carry on in the vain hope that they will wake up and suddenly discover just how interesting you are being. Pause. Wait until one or two faces look towards you in puzzlement and then carry on. Alternatively, try speaking more quietly – this may make the delegates concentrate so that they can hear you. Or just give the delegates a five-minute break. Whatever you choose to do, the aim is to vary the pace. Speaking in the same tone or for more than a few minutes at a time will invariably result in some loss of your students' attention.

Of course, it is far better to plan and deliver your training session with the aim of avoiding boredom. Adding in different exercises and activities will help you to vary the pace and this should, of course, be done at the planning stage (we looked at this in Chapter 6). During this stage you will have made sure that you are never standing in front of the delegates delivering an over-long presentation but will have planned in a variety of delivery methods such as syndicate exercises, quizzes, brainstorming sessions, video material and discussions.

While you are planning your presentation, you will probably also be preparing notes for yourself to keep you on track. Notes are invaluable (even Winston Churchill used notes) as few people can deliver a complete course without at least a few reminders of where they are going and how they are going to get there. Do be sensible in your use of notes. They are there as reminders rather than as a script so do not read directly from them. Delegates will rarely appreciate being read to!

Body language

We've looked briefly at how you can tell if your delegates are getting bored, but what else can we tell from body language? Like verbal communication and feedback, body language works two ways. If you are able to control your own body language and, at the same time, read the body language of your audience, then your communication skills will improve, making it easier to get your message across. It has been said that over half of our understanding comes from non-verbal communication, so we do need to be aware of body language – even if we have designed a perfect set of course materials and have an ideal set of delegates!

To explore the use of body language to any great extent would be the subject of another book, but there are undoubtedly a few simple things that you can do to gain some benefit from being aware of body language:

The delegates' body language

Reading the body language of your delegates can be helpful in directing your presentation and dealing with possible problems. It can also form part of your strategy to evaluate their performance during your training sessions. Let's look at some of the aspects you may notice and what they might mean in terms of how they are receiving the information you are giving them:

- Delegates leaning forward in their seats – lucky you! You've got some delegates who are paying attention and are eager to learn.
- Delegates slouching in their seats – this could mean problems. It could signify a variety of negative responses to your presentation or it could just mean that they are tired or uninterested. It could also mean that the delegate in question is unable to cope with the material so be aware of this possibility. In any event you will have to work hard to get their attention and to ensure that you meet your learning objectives.
- Delegates not making eye contact – this could just be shyness or it could signify a lack of empathy. If they are, instead, looking around the room then this almost certainly signifies

boredom. Maybe they are wishing they weren't there.

- Facial expression – this is very important. It is usually easy to discern boredom or interest, or to see if delegates look distressed or display a lack of understanding.
- Open or closed bodies – if delegates are sitting with their arms crossed in front of their bodies, or have their hands on their faces or over their mouths, then they are displaying closed behaviour; this means that they will be unlikely to take in everything you are saying. Open behaviour, on the other hand, with their faces towards you, perhaps nodding to show their understanding, and their arms by their sides or on the desks, will show that they are open to what you are saying and are willing to learn.

When everyone has settled for your opening session, look around. Notice whether everyone looks comfortable but alert. Repeat this at the start of each session and use it to keep a running check on who is concentrating and who is not. If you feel that some delegates are failing to make contact with you, make sure that you ask them a question or try to draw them into any discussion sessions. Also use the information that your careful observation provides to help you decide who should be put into groups with whom for syndicate exercises. Aim for a balance of types. Don't put all the eager, willing-to-learn delegates together. The able trainees will help the more reluctant or less confident ones to learn. This will promote team-working and will make your syndicate exercises work much better.

Your own body language

If you are totally unaware of the non-verbal messages that you are giving out, then you could – if that message is fear or incompetence – lose your audience before you have said a single word. If, however, you can gain the support of your delegates right at the start of your presentation with confident, encouraging body language, you will find that you will have a much easier time. Your aim should be to establish a rapport with the delegates as soon as you can and to put them at their ease so that they are ready to learn with you and from you. Some ways you can try to do this are:

- Stand up – even if you have planned your room set-up so that you are sitting with your delegates during a lot of your training event, do not sit down until you have delivered your opener. Standing up gives you a position of authority and influence. Don't slouch or keep your head down. Your posture affects your presentation and how your voice carries. Try to position yourself so that you can be seen by all the delegates and that their view of you is not ruined by light streaming through a window or your flipchart being in the way.

- Speak up – make sure that all the delegates can hear you clearly. You might want to check early on in your opening session that everyone can hear and is paying attention by asking a question.
- Look up – do not speak to the floor or the wall at the back of the room. Make eye contact with several delegates but don't stare to the point that you make someone uncomfortable.
- Move but don't fidget – move around sometimes, but not continuously. If you've been standing in one spot for a while, walk across the room, but if you find yourself pacing about, stand still. A change like this will help to keep your delegates' attention. Be aware of all the things that you might do that are distracting – rocking backwards and forwards, jingling change in your pocket, tapping a pen on the desk, etc.

Discussion – should you lead it or follow it?

Discussion is a powerful aid to learning so it is a desirable element of almost any training course. However, discussions should not be allowed to descend into aimless chat or to ramble into irrelevant areas. A presenter who includes discussion time in a training event needs to know the subject extremely well as the discussion may roam around the subject in a way that may be difficult to follow and, just as importantly, to keep on track so that the specific aims of the session are achieved. If you're planning a discussion session in your course, consider how many delegates you will have. Too few and discussion may be difficult and stilted with too few opinions being aired for consideration. Too many and the session could become disorganized and difficult to follow, or some delegates may not get the opportunity to express opinions adequately. At its best, discussion can produce a satisfying session where learning is reinforced, but at its worst you will waste time and achieve little.

The main choice is whether to lead a discussion or to allow your delegates to go where the discussion takes them and you merely follow. This is the choice between controlled discussion that follows the plans of the trainer and open discussion where delegates' priorities are paramount. While open discussion can generate ideas and help teams to work together, you would be unwise to use this method unless the creativity and teamwork that it can foster are high on your list of learning objectives. Controlled discussion, on the other hand, can enliven a session while creating greater understanding of the subject matter and at the same time can encompass the advantages of open discussion – teamwork and creativity.

In planning a discussion as part of your training session you should be careful that you know exactly what you hope to achieve and you should set a strict time limit for it. You should be prepared to lead the discussion so that it goes in your planned direction and that the pace keeps you on track with regard to your objectives and time limit. A list of the points that you aim to cover during the discussion will be useful for you. You may also find it helpful to set a few ground rules, such as that no one should interrupt or be allowed to dominate a discussion to the exclusion of others who want to speak, and that everyone presenting ideas should be prepared to justify and explain. Properly run, a discussion can have the following advantages:

- promotes better team-working
- can be used to change attitudes
- promotes analytical thinking
- builds on communication skills
- ideas can be exchanged and developed
- adds variety to the training

Be aware of the disadvantages also:

- requires in-depth knowledge on the part of the trainer
- worthwhile discussion can take up a lot of time in a training session
- it is not easy to facilitate and control a discussion
- pre-existing conflicts within the group may affect the outcome

Your job as discussion leader will be to keep control of the proceedings and ensure that the objective is met. You will find it easier to keep control if you are at the front of the group with everyone facing towards you but also able to see each other clearly. You will need to start the discussion by presenting a carefully composed question. You should then try to ensure that everyone has a chance to contribute early in the discussion by asking open questions that you will have prepared in advance.

During the discussion you should actively listen and observe the delegates and make sure that you draw out the information that is necessary according to your learning objectives for the session. Try to summarize the information and ideas as you go along and get agreement from the delegates about their understanding of the issues. Make sure that you facilitate a controlled argument and draw out any views that have not been aired. Keep an eye on the time so that the discussion does not get out of hand and be careful to avoid a contentious or new issue being raised when you are coming to the end of the allotted time.

Although a good, productive discussion will probably have no shortage of contributors, there will no doubt come a time when the pace slows and there is a lull in the proceedings. Do not be tempted to intervene too quickly. Allow them all some thinking time and then start to ask questions. Aim them at people who have previously made valid contributions so that you can get the discussion back on its feet. If you leap in too soon and supply the answers, the delegates could become lazy and allow you to provide them with all the answers rather than reasoning out some of the points in the discussion for themselves.

If you have facilitated an effective discussion session, the result should be a set of conclusions and a summary of the main points raised. The delegates should benefit from a tightly controlled discussion that promotes creativity and teamwork and makes them question their own views as well as those of the other delegates. One last piece of advice – do not let the discussion get personal at any point.

Dealing with questions

Decide in advance whether you are prepared to take questions during your presentation or would prefer to keep them until the end of the session. At the beginning of your training event advise your delegates of your preference. There are, of course, advantages and disadvantages to both ways, but if you opt for taking questions throughout the session, you will need to be confident and strong in order to keep the presentation on track. However, if you can manage this, you could use questions to break up a long presentation and they can be used as an opportunity to check understanding as you go along. They can then be used to reinforce and further explain complicated points. You may also find that you will get fewer questions if you keep them to the end of the session as delegates may forget what they had intended to ask, or they may not want to delay their departure at the end of the day by engaging in questions.

When asking for questions, make sure that you use open questions. For example, ask 'What questions do you have?' rather than 'Anybody got any questions?' Make eye contact with a few delegates, especially anyone who looks alert and curious so that you can get the question-and-answer session going. The first question is always the most difficult to elicit, so try to look enthusiastic rather than worried!

When you get your first question, take a breath – a quick and maybe glib answer will not win any prizes. Make sure that everyone heard and understood the question before you give them your considered reply (it can be helpful to rephrase it) and try to link your answer to points that you have made in your presentation. Don't make your answer too long – hopefully there will be several other questioners eager to get in on the act.

You will find this part of the session easier if you try to anticipate the kind of questions that you will be asked and have prepared some points that you want to include in your answers. Use this to the full, as it is an opportunity to reinforce points and to ensure that you meet your training objectives.

Always keep your course objectives in mind and try to ensure that irrelevant or awkward questions do not take you down inappropriate avenues. If a question is asked that threatens your aims for that particular session, acknowledge the question but suggest that you come back to it later or that you will speak to the questioner later – over coffee, for example.

You may be relieved when your delegates come up with some questions but, rest assured, there will be some awkward ones amongst them. Even if the questioner is intent on scoring a point or is inarticulate – or has simply misunderstood something – you should avoid the temptation to embarrass them. Keep your cool and rephrase the question so that it is useful to the session.

What can you do if there are no questions? It could be your worst nightmare – you've come to the end of the session and asked, 'What questions do you have?' and you are met with silence. The ideal would be to have asked for written questions in advance and then select from these to illustrate the main points from the session. If you haven't done this then you will need to ad-lib a little. You may say, 'I thought I would have been asked . . .', or ask the delegates a question of your own. Reassure them that if they have something they didn't understand, then someone else will certainly have the same problem.

TRAINING TIP
Try to use each question as an opportunity to reinforce points from your session.

Summary

- Practise the opening to each session so that you feel comfortable.
- Make a good first impression by making delegates welcome, starting on time, making eye contact and stating your learning objectives clearly.
- A good presenter is one who is comfortable, confident and well organized and who knows his audience.
- Being aware of your own body language and that of your delegates can greatly improve your presentation skills.
- Vary the pace to avoid delegates becoming bored.
- Well-controlled discussions can be used to reinforce objectives and develop ideas.
- Decide in advance when you want delegates to ask questions.

Revision test

1. Apart from the trainer's confidence and knowledge of his audience, what is a vital characteristic of a good presentation?
2. Name three signs that delegates are listening during a training session.
3. How much of our understanding is estimated to come from non-verbal communication?
4. If presenters want to project authority and influence, should they stand up or sit down?
5. Name two possible ground rules that could be set to ensure an effective discussion during a training session.
6. What reassurance can you offer delegates if they do not come up with any questions when you have asked for them?

7 Name two ways that you can make your objectives known at the start of a training session.
8 What can a presenter use, rather than reading out extensive notes, to keep to the planned session?
9 Name three delivery methods to avoid boredom in training sessions.
10 Describe closed behaviour in terms of body language.

In this chapter you will:

- look at the various types of visual aids that are available
- learn when is best to use the aids – and when not to . . .

Different types

Visual aids are an extremely important part of a training course. It has been proved that people remember far more information (approximately three times as much) when they can both see and hear the information than when they are merely listening. Used in the right way and at the right time, visual aids can help to make sense of difficult concepts and can reinforce ideas. For example, a video demonstrating how to deal with a customer complaint, perhaps with a touch of humour to illustrate what not to do, can get a very important message across.

There are several different types of visual aid for use in training sessions:

- flipcharts
- overhead projectors (OHPs) with transparencies
- 35mm slides
- laptop presentations
- video/DVD presentations
- real objects – such as sample products, machines, photographs or models

All of these types of visual aid will help you to get your message across and all have their advantages and disadvantages so let's look at them one by one:

Flipcharts

This is the visual aid that is most likely to be available and is the single most useful visual aid for any trainer. It is also the lowest cost and needs no power – just remember to ensure that good quality markers in a variety of easy-to-see colours are available and that you have a spare pad to hand. Despite its apparent simplicity, it can be daunting to write on a flipchart in front of a roomful of delegates. Getting the size of your writing just right, keeping it straight rather than writing diagonally across the page, and making sure that everyone can read what you have written – even at the back of the room – can be surprisingly difficult. So, unless you are very confident, practise a lot beforehand or prepare written sheets for the flipchart in advance. If you know in advance what points you want to make (you do, don't you?) and also how you want to illustrate them, then pre-prepared flipcharts will save you time, potential pitfalls, and possible embarrassment during your presentation. Flipcharts have an added advantage in that they can present good opportunities for audience participation.

Tips for using flipcharts

- prepare in advance so that you can avoid major mistakes while you are presenting
- add minor elements to your pre-prepared sheets as you display them to give an active feel to your presentation
- use easy-to-read colours – black and blue are best for the bulk of the writing, but an extra colour can be useful to highlight important points
- avoid permanent markers – water soluble markers do not show through on the sheets underneath
- use letters at least 2.5cm high to make them possible to read – obviously the further away the delegates are from the chart, the bigger the writing needs to be
- leave a blank sheet between each pre-prepared page that you can turn to as soon as you have finished making the point shown on the written page – this avoids leaving the page that you have just dealt with visible to the delegates (or worse, turning the page and exposing the next stage of your presentation); both of these scenarios are extremely distracting
- try not to turn your back on the delegates for too long while you are writing
- make sure you have a spare pad for the flipchart
- practise using a flipchart before the training event – it is not unknown for an inexperienced presenter to freeze when faced with a big blank page or for the writing to be so small as to cause amusement, or for the flipchart to collapse! Better for all these problems to occur in private

Overhead projectors with transparencies

Overhead projectors (OHPs) are often available and produce a large, clear image without the need for putting out the lights in the room. This is a great advantage as it enables you to keep making eye contact with the trainees and to ensure that their attention is being retained. An OHP is portable and you can produce high-quality transparencies relatively easily using a computer.

Tips for using OHPs

- position the OHP carefully in advance of your presentation – make sure that it does not obscure the delegates' view of you
- use colour – this is easy with a colour printer or coloured pens specially produced for this purpose

- check in advance that your transparencies are readable when projected
- only display the transparencies when you want them to be the focus of attention; when you've dealt with the topic on a transparency take it away and move on – leaving it displayed will distract your audience
- stand to the right of the screen so that you do not block your audience's view; because we read from left to right, the right hand side of the screen is a good place to stand, as the delegates' eyes will naturally move to you when they have finished reading
- keep your transparencies in order both before and after you have displayed them; keep the used ones and the ones still to come separate so that you don't get confused
- make sure that you – or someone who is easily available during your presentation – knows how to change the bulb
- practise using an OHP so that you do not have to keep checking the position of the transparency and that you can change them smoothly – fumbling is always a distraction

35mm slides

These are starting to lose popularity but are still readily available. When the initial effort and outlay has been made to develop a set of high-quality slides, they are often used over and over again.

Tips for using 35mm slides

- make sure that the room is dark enough to see the slides clearly
- arrange in advance for someone to be responsible for turning the lights on and off
- try to group slides together for display so that you do not have to adjust the lighting too frequently
- don't make the slides too fussy – beware of mixing font styles and sizes and of putting too many words on each slide
- do not use too many slides or change them too frequently; give your audience time to see and absorb each slide – a minimum of 60 to 90 seconds each
- don't try to include too much information on each slide – there is a limit to how much information can be absorbed
- don't forget to use just one point per slide and do remember that if you need to explain where to find the point of the slide, then the slide is wrong – throw it out or redo it!

- a remote control to change the slides is useful as it is less distracting and allows you to stand out of the way of the projection
- try to site the projector at the back of the room, away from the delegates, to minimize noise problems
- have a back-up plan (a flipchart or a standby projector, for example) as projectors frequently go wrong
- decide in advance where you will stand; don't stand between the projector and the screen (ever!) and don't stand between the delegates and the screen – the best place, if you are right-handed, is just to the right of the screen
- face the delegates as much as possible during your slide show – if you turn towards the screen, they will find it difficult to hear you
- remove a slide from display as soon as you have finished with it to avoid distracting your audience
- check – and double check – that all your slides are the right way up!

Laptop presentations

If you are confident of your ability to use the equipment associated with a presentation on a laptop computer, these can be very effective. However, a common equipment malfunction is that the remote control for changing the slides has a slight delay and it can be difficult to recover composure after making a mess of the slide changes. You should also be proficient in the use of PowerPoint software although someone else could, of course, prepare them for you when you have written them. In this case make sure that you have checked them – and checked them again – and that you are familiar with how to go backwards and forwards through the presentation.

Some tips for using PowerPoint

- decide upon an overall theme (including colours and fonts to be used) for the appearance of your slides so that your presentation will have a pleasing, uniform look
- ensure that your theme does not use too many colours, make sure the colours don't clash and that there is sufficient contrast between the colours used to give an easily visible image on the screen
- do not make your theme too fussy – it will detract from the point you are trying to make
- make a master slide using your theme

- limit yourself to just one main point per slide
- have a run-through of the complete presentation on PowerPoint so that you are familiar with it and are sure that the order is correct
- use charts and graphs to demonstrate points and to present statistical information – they will be far easier to understand than using figures in tables
- try to search out some new graphics to use – some popular graphics will have been seen so often by your delegates that they will not enhance your presentation at all
- make a list of everything you need to take – the laptop, the disk containing the presentation, the projector, cables, battery and your notes
- don't forget that you can print out your notes from the PowerPoint presentation for use during the session

TRAINING TIP

Make sure that you have a back-up. Take a spare copy of the presentation with you and also think about how you will deliver the presentation if you have a technical failure of some sort.

Video/DVD

Professionally made videos or DVD presentations can be extremely effective but they must, of course, be genuinely relevant to your course. Used correctly, a video can break up a long presentation and provide light-relief for both the presenter and the delegates whilst imparting useful knowledge and illustrating points you have made. It can be the most complete, ready-made presentation available – possibly having pictures, words, demonstrations, music, highly professional presenters – and is a timed presentation that uses relatively simple equipment.

Using videos effectively requires planning. You must ensure that you have the correct equipment – a television screen of adequate size, sited so that all delegates have a good view of it. You should also ensure that the sound quality is sufficient for the room you are using. The video to be used should be inserted in the machine before the session begins and rewound to the starting point required. You really cannot avoid the necessity to check a video in advance – check its content, volume settings and quality (don't forget that repeated copying means that the quality of a video will deteriorate). This checking will also ensure that you are familiar with both the video and the equipment.

Real objects – such as sample products, photographs or models

Physical objects can be a very useful and effective way of getting an idea across and can also brighten up a dull presentation. They can give a feeling of reality to an abstract idea.

If you are conducting a practical session, for example, on the use of a new item of equipment or on the benefits of a new product, you will find it useful to have an example of the equipment or product available. Don't forget that although you may be very familiar with an object, the delegates may not be, so the inner workings of a machine, for example, can be explained very effectively by producing a stripped down version of it.

Being able to touch something is a powerful aid to learning, but great care must be taken that the object is relevant and also that it is presented at the right time. It can be very distracting to have objects passed around during your presentation. Your delegates' attention will be on the object or a discussion about the object rather than what you are saying, so beware.

When to use them and when not to . . .

Visual aids of all types will be useful when used in the right way at the right time. Remember that visual aids are just that – aids. You should not decide upon them first and build your presentation around them. Do it the other way round – plan your sessions, ensure the structure of the entire event is balanced and only then start to assess what visual aids would enhance your presentation. The key word here is 'enhance' – the addition of any visual aids should improve your presentation and help towards achieving your training objectives. Here are some dos and don'ts:

- **Do** use visual aids when they enhance your message. They will break up your presentation, helping to avoid boredom amongst your delegates and also making it easier to understand.
- **Do not** use poor quality visual aids. Slides, for example, should be easy to read and have an obvious message. If they are difficult to read or contain too much information, revise

them – they will only detract from your message. Better slides will help you to get your message across.

- **Do not** use visual aids when they are irrelevant – they may be full of fancy effects or technical wizardry, but if they do not help in achieving your learning objective, leave them out. And while we're on the subject of technical wizardry, don't get carried away because then all the delegates will see are the special effects that you have used rather than your message.
- **Do not** use visual aids if you are not familiar with the equipment. You will not get your delegates to learn anything while you are fiddling with the OHP, trying to find the ON switch. You must familiarize yourself with all the equipment well before the training session and practise, practise, practise.
- **Do not** use too many visual aids. Try to strike a balance between using aids, such as videos and slides, and exercises that the delegates can get involved in. Sitting and watching can become boring.

Top tips for preparing visual aids

- do use visual aids – they will improve your delegates' level of understanding and retention
- don't make them too complicated – if your audience is fascinated by the graphics and animation, they may miss your real message
- use visual aids to help you to break up the monotony for the delegates – and for you
- don't merely present pages of written information copied on to acetates. This is unimaginative, difficult to see, and can be daunting for delegates
- use bullet-pointed lists
- don't put lots of numbers on a visual aid – far better to present numerical information in the form of a graph or chart
- make your visual aids tidy and legible – too many words are difficult to digest
- do not put any unnecessary information – such as your company logo or the date that you prepared a slide – on any visual aids – it will detract from your message; everything on the slide should be there for a purpose – it should illustrate, explain or reinforce the point that you are trying to get across
- take care that the information you present with your visual aids is not too complicated – if you have to explain the information on a slide, for example, then it needs simplifying

- use colour in your slides to increase attention span – different coloured fonts can improve your visual aids, but remember not to make them too busy
- do choose the right sort of font for your slides: sans serif fonts – the ones without the little feet to connect the letters – such as Arial, make slides easier to read from a distance (this is another reason why you should not merely photocopy pages from your notes onto slides); serif fonts, such as Times New Roman, are ideal for notes and books but a different approach is needed for slides
- don't use a visual aid unless you are certain that it will improve that particular part of your presentation
- do practise using visual aids before presenting the course
- don't forget to check any machines – laptop, OHP, pointing devices, etc. – immediately before each session; the failure of bulbs and electrical connections during a session is very distracting and, in my experience as both a delegate and a presenter, is more common than you might think
- do use real objects – touch is a powerful learning medium
- don't hand round product samples or other objects during your presentation as this will merely distract your audience; plan their use carefully (this also applies to written handouts)

Summary

- Visual aids can be a valuable addition to a training session if they are used judiciously – remember that, above all, they must be relevant.
- There are a variety of visual aids that all have their place to illustrate presentations and to reinforce learning.
- Trainees retain approximately three times more information when they see and hear it compared with when they are just listening.
- Trying to include too much information on a slide or transparency is the most common error made when preparing visual aids.
- Whichever visual aids you use, practise using them until you are confident.
- Visual aids will help your presentation – they will create interest and add variety and impact while furthering your delegates' understanding.

Revision test

1 Which visual aid has the lowest cost and is most commonly available?
2 What can you do to avoid making major mistakes during your presentation using a flipchart?
3 What should you do – and why – when you've dealt with a topic shown on a transparency?
4 What back-up plans could you have in case the projector doesn't work during a presentation?
5 How many main points per slide is recommended?
6 List three things that you should take with you when you are doing a laptop presentation.
7 What do you need to check before using a video for the first time?
8 When should you plan your visual aids?
9 How can visual aids help your presentation?
10 When should you avoid handing out product samples, written notes or other objects?

09 dealing with different learning types

In this chapter you will:

- **discover the different learning styles**
- **look at how you can deal with the many types of people that you may encounter**
- **learn how to stay focused despite interruptions**

Different learning styles

You will find that there is a variety of learning styles within any group of people and you must ensure that your training event encompasses different ways of putting the information across so that you cater for all of these. For example, some people can learn easily by listening to the trainer and reflecting upon what they have been told, while others need some 'hands-on' experience to enable them to fully understand the training. With these two types and others to cater for in designing your training sessions, you should include some sessions where the trainer delivers training by standing in front of the group and telling them the details of what he wants them to know as well as sessions that involve some exercises that are based on real-life situations. In this latter case, you might include some real objects such as product samples or photographs and also some role-play to get this type of learner involved. Now that you have seen that each group will include a cross-section of learning styles and that these styles demand different ways of delivering training to get the most out of the event, we can look at the main learning styles in more detail and at which ways of delivery will suit them best.

The Innovative Type

This type of person is likely to be easy-going and will listen to the trainer – and to others – before using their imagination to come up with lots of different solutions to the problem in hand. They will ask questions, share ideas and will also try to involve others in the group before reaching a conclusion. They do not like conflict and will need to be actively involved in a training session.

If only all delegates could be like this. They will listen when you are delivering a lecture-type session and will ask questions when they need to. They will also play an active part in any syndicate exercises, coming up with innovative suggestions but without monopolizing your time so that everyone can make a contribution.

The Analytical Type

This learning style shows itself in the need to think through any idea or concept that is presented to them. The analytical type is likely to be cool and unemotional and will be more interested in ideas and data than in people. They need to be presented with facts, figures and lots of detail that they will then analyse, compare with past experiences and put into order before putting together an organized plan. They are usually hardworking and always organized.

The analytical learner will need plenty of facts and figures to work on so for this type of delegate you must ensure that your handouts include plenty of information and that you provide exercises that make full use of their analytical powers.

The Passive Type

These are the people who will sit and listen patiently and may have the ability to absorb new information without seeming to make any effort. They will usually, however, be very self-disciplined and will always comply with instructions and be able to meet even the tightest of deadlines. They may be closely allied to the analytical type but may frustrate the trainer and the other members of their group by their lack of involvement and seeming lack of effort. Their controlled approach to learning can disguise a person who plans carefully and is good at the administrative side of many tasks so, despite their distant manner, they can be a useful member of any team.

This type of learner may cause some concern for you as the trainer, who may be confused by their quiet, uninvolved manner. When you notice this sort of behaviour, you should ascertain for yourself that this type of delegate has not got any problem with the course material and then, apart from ensuring that they are playing their part in any joint exercises and asking them the occasional question, you should leave them to their own devices.

The Risk-taker

This type of learning style manifests itself as someone who is perhaps quick to get involved and to make decisions (sometimes too quick) and acts on hunches rather than detailed information. Their decisions are often right without their having any logical explanation for that decision and this can be frustrating and perplexing for the analytical types. Both types need to be exposed to the alternative method of reaching decisions so do not make any attempt to keep these types apart – they can form a mutually beneficial partnership. The risk-taker is enthusiastic and sociable so is a useful team member – especially if you have a number of shy or uninterested members in your group. They deal in feelings, hunches and opinion rather than facts, figures and detail.

The aspect of the risk-taker's learning style that you need to beware of is their speed. You could find that they are impatient to move the session along so that other slower delegates, maybe more analytical in their approach, are frustrated and may not get the maximum benefit from the session. The risk-takers must be held back so that the others can be allowed to reach their own conclusions and to assimilate the knowledge that they are being given. It might also be useful to take one of the quicker delegate's decisions and analyse, with the risk-taker's help, how they could have arrived at their conclusion. This type of situation could develop into an interesting discussion if well led by the trainer, and can be a satisfying learning experience for everyone.

The Hands-on Type

This member of your team needs to see examples of the point you are trying to get across and will look for proof and usefulness for any topic. They will try to find out how things work in real life and will search out results and practical solutions. You will find that this type will be good at solving problems and will use a common sense approach. Quite often they will ask a question but not expect a direct answer from you, as they want to discover, and prove, the solution for themselves.

The material that you include for the hands-on learning type must include plenty of case studies and examples taken from real work situations so that they can see how what they are being told will apply and how they can use the knowledge that is on offer. They may particularly appreciate training videos.

You should appreciate that no particular type is always preferable or superior – they are just different – and there will usually be a blend of these learning styles in any group of delegates. You will therefore need to ensure that any training event is planned to include sessions that cater for all the styles. This means including some listening sessions, some written information, some hands-on experience in the form of syndicate exercises or practical experience of a skill and some exercises that require an analytical approach. Try to be aware of the learning styles you have in your group and mix these up for syndicate exercises so that each group will have a blend of skills available to them. In this way, each group member will have the opportunity to experience, and gain benefit from, a variety of capabilities in their fellow team members.

Keeping your goals in sight

It is you – the trainer – who has set the objectives for your training event and it is your responsibility to ensure that these objectives are met. You will come across various difficult trainees who will, either by design or by accident, disrupt your training sessions. Don't be disheartened, as these people are in the minority – the majority of trainees are usually ready, willing and able to participate fully in the training that you are offering them. There are a few who will resent having to attend any training or who don't care whether they have to attend or not but, as you will see below, there are ways that you can overcome the difficulties that all the different types will cause. The important thing to remember is not to take any of the criticism or awkwardness personally and to keep your learning objectives in sight. As we have discussed previously, you should display your aims for the course or the session prominently at the start of each session and also make sure that all the delegates have been informed of your expectations of them with regard to questions and behaviour.

Sometimes you will be able to spot straight away the delegates who are out to cause trouble, or those who are going to have difficulty meeting your training objectives. If the delegates are all known to you in advance, or you have done your research and checked out their aptitudes and attitudes with their line manager in advance of the course (but do not let this research degenerate into a gossiping session – just find out the essentials that might affect your event), then you will have a head start. When you know where the problems are, you will be able to deal with them. Having identified a possible problem, you can pay special attention early on in the course so that you can get that person actively involved – perhaps ask him or her a question about what they already know about the subject of the training, or plan to put them into a group or pairing for a syndicate exercise with someone who will counter the difficulty in their personality.

Next we will look at the three main groups of difficult delegates that you may encounter.

Hecklers, know-it-alls and talkative types

In this group we find people who like to make their presence felt. The first of these – the heckler – is mercifully rare. For a new trainer the person who shouts out disruptive, and often insulting, remarks can be very difficult to deal with. It is usually impossible to ignore a heckler so you should give some consideration to how you would deal with their noisy interruptions. The first advice is, as always, not to take their behaviour personally. Instead, you need to attempt to find out the root of their problem (and ultimately it is their problem, not yours). If they are dissatisfied with the training that they are receiving, try to resolve the difficulty on the spot. If this is not possible, offer to speak with them after the session has finished and if necessary let them leave the session. Do not allow disruption of the training to go on.

The know-it-alls are not as difficult to deal with as the hecklers but they are more common. Sometimes the problem can be diffused by giving them the recognition they crave. Acknowledge the knowledge that they are displaying and move on. Keep in control of the session by then avoiding their questions and comments if possible, by concentrating on more reticent delegates. You might also find it helpful to pair the know-it-all with someone who needs help with the material.

Delegates who talk too much – usually chatting amongst themselves – can be dealt with by drawing attention to them. They often aren't aware just how disruptive their chattering is. Walk over to the chatterer and wait nearby until you have their attention, then carry on with the session. If the room layout does not allow this, you could try looking at them without saying anything or ask them if they have a question for you.

Whichever of these disruptive types you come across, the aim should be the same – do not allow them to take over or disrupt your session, as it should remain in your control the whole time if you are to have a chance of meeting your objectives.

The shy, the anxious and the overwhelmed

The main issue with this group is in identifying the cause of their problem. If a delegate is not making any contribution to the session – never coming up with any questions, comments or answers – then you will need to decide just exactly what is the problem. It may be that they know the answer to a question but are too shy to offer their contribution, or they could be just naturally worried, anxious or lacking in confidence. They could also be overwhelmed by the session and not really up to the level of learning and interaction expected. If you decide that the delegate is either shy or anxious then you will need to attempt to instil some confidence in them and draw them out so that they play at least a small part in the course. Find an easy question to direct to them. Avoid negative comments, try to act in a friendly manner and encourage them with your body language.

The overwhelmed must be dealt with in a different way. It may be necessary for them to be removed from the course if you are unable to involve them in the session in a productive yet comfortable way. If you decide that they are unable to cope with the session or that they will not be able to meet the learning objectives of the course then this may be the only option. However, before you reach this conclusion do make sure that you have tried, with encouraging behaviour, positive body language and, if it is acceptable to the troubled delegate, the offer of a little extra help with explanations of the materials.

The uninterested

This final category of difficult delegate could be mistaken for those who are shy or anxious, but there is a much more difficult problem to solve if you meet a delegate who is just uninterested in the course. They feel that they shouldn't be there, that it is not worth the effort and that anyone who is showing any enthusiasm must be mad. So, what can you do with these people?

The first thing is to ascertain whether lack of interest and commitment is the problem rather than anxiousness or feeling that they cannot cope with the level of the course. You should be able to spot the signs of a lack of interest – restlessness, lack of participation, doing as they are instructed but with little enthusiasm or commitment and answering questions in a perfunctory manner with little thought and throwaway lines.

Next you will need to consider the person's learning style (see the section above for more details) and motivation. Their motivation, which could be about status or perceived lack of rewards or benefits of the training, will be important in determining how you treat the uninterested delegate. If you can start to motivate them you will have done a good job.

In addition to their motivation, your learning objectives will also be important. Explain what you expect them to gain from the training and explore whether or not they share these aims in any way (and if not, why not?). Do they see the value of learning one or more of the particular topics covered by the training? Can they relate it to their job? Try to gain commitment from the uninterested delegate to at least some part of your aims and request that they move forward in the training on this basis.

Your aim in respect of this type of problem should be to get the delegate actively involved in your training session. Another way in which you might do this is to nominate them to help others if you feel that they already have some of the skills that you are training. In this way, they may learn – or at least have their skills consolidated – without realizing that they are doing so.

Whoever you come across, try to ensure that you do not spend a disproportionate amount of time on any of these difficult characters. Your key responsibility is to the group and if you do consider changing your style, your timing or the content of the course, this must only be done if the benefits you gain are in proportion to the effort and disruption. Remember that you are aiming at a 'best fit' between the group's needs and the training you are offering. Obtaining perfection, with everyone getting the maximum benefit from the training, may be impossible.

Whatever the type of difficult delegate you come up against, do not allow them to hijack your training session. You should, of course, try to ensure that each and every delegate makes the most of the training opportunity but do not allow one 'rogue' trainee to divert your attention too much. You must remain in control. This is essential not just for the good of the course and the majority of (willing) learners but also for your own peace of mind. If you are seen to be weak or distracted, you will be in danger of losing the respect of the delegates and you will certainly risk becoming less effective.

Summary

- You will find a variety of learning styles in any group of delegates.
- The Innovative Type will listen, ask questions and come up with ideas. They need only be encouraged.
- The Analytical Type will be interested in ideas and data so make sure that they have plenty of facts and figures to work with.
- The Passive Type will appear uninvolved but will be benefiting from the training and can be a good team member for syndicate exercises.
- The Risk-taker will make quick decisions and sometimes needs help to understand how to analyse their conclusions.
- The Hands-on Type will need realistic examples of the way that the points they are learning can be used.
- You may meet many difficult delegates but you must keep your objectives in sight. Try to find out what their problem is and deal with it straight away.
- Do not let any one delegate hijack your training session. Stay in control.

Revision test

1 Which learning style is likely to be cool and unemotional and needs to think through ideas and concepts?
2 Which visual aid might be particularly appreciated by a 'Hands-On' learning type?
3 What should be a trainer's aim in dealing with hecklers, know-it-alls and talkative types?
4 How might a trainer help a delegate who is overwhelmed by the course?
5 What are the signs to look for that show a lack of interest on the part of a delegate?
6 Which learning type is likely to listen, ask questions, come up with ideas and be active in your training sessions?
7 How does a 'Risk Taker' make decisions?
8 Which learning type seems to be able to take in information without making an effort?
9 Name two ways that a trainer could supply information to an analytical delegate.
10 Give two important things to remember when faced with criticism or awkwardness from delegates.

In this chapter you will:

- **find out how to design exercises to evaluate the training as it happens**
- **get tips on how to give – and receive – feedback**

Why evaluate?

Training of any type – good or bad – is expensive, time consuming and demanding. So it is essential to be sure that the results are worth the effort. Most of the formal evaluation will take place, as we shall see in Chapter 11, after the training event is over when you will be able to see the results of the training in use back in the workplace. Although this post-training evaluation is vital and will help to ensure that you get an appropriate return on your investment in training, it is also carried out too late to alter the results of any particular training session. You must therefore be prepared to continually assess how the training is going during the sessions and to adjust your approach accordingly. Although questionnaires, tests and surveys carried out when the delegates have left the training venue will help you to prove whether or not the training has been successful (and can be used to improve training events in the future and to influence decisions as to the training policy of your organization), evaluation while delegates are still in front of the trainer is also essential.

If you can develop strategies and methods that will help you, as the trainer or the training co-ordinator, to assess the effectiveness of your training sessions during the event, you will have the opportunity to put right some of the problems you may discover. You should be able to note where extra attention is needed and then to tweak your summing-up sessions so that the problem areas are reinforced. There are many ways in which you can evaluate during training sessions ranging from informal methods, such as observing the delegates, to more formal testing methods. We will look next at some of the ways in which you can assess progress while you still have the chance to put things right.

Appropriate questioning

The development of an evaluation strategy, including appropriate questions to be planned in advance of the session, should take into account the type of training being given and also the type of skill being trained. For instance, a functional skill such as product assembly or driving a forklift truck will be tested at the end of the session using a practical test and perhaps just a few questions will be needed. During the session you may ask a driver about maintenance procedures, for example, or an assembly worker may be questioned about the various product faults he may encounter. However, the most important aspect of this type of training is that the trainee develops a practical skill that can be tested in practical ways. In the case of more academic training sessions, there will usually be plenty of opportunity – and need – for questioning throughout the training.

The type of training also dictates to some extent the appropriate time and way to ask questions. A trainer conducting training sessions involving slides will need to have questions prepared for the end of that session so that he can evaluate whether or not the delegates have taken in the important points in the slides and that they will be able to use the knowledge in the future (thus showing that the session has met its objectives). A different type of training – for example, online training to improve customer service skills – will demand a different way of assessment. Training using a PC can be used to repeat a point as often as necessary and a way of assessing whether or not the point has been assimilated will be built into the software program. This will mean that questions from anyone else during such a session are often unnecessary.

Questions during training sessions are mainly used to evaluate the ongoing effectiveness of the training but they can also be useful in maintaining the focus of the session (and of the delegates!), encouraging thinking, delving deeper into the issues under discussion and in providing a link to the next topic in the session. However, by far the most important use of questions is that of evaluation, so here are some tips on developing and using appropriate questions:

- Prepare your questions in advance. As you plan each training session, think of questions that will test your delegates' understanding of the principles you are trying to convey.
- Ask open questions. Don't ask, 'Do you understand that?' or 'Is that clear?' but instead ask, 'What do you understand from that?' or 'How will that affect the way you do your job?'
- Make your questions specific and make sure that you ask the right question. You must be clear exactly what information you are trying to extract from your trainees and tailor your question to fit the situation.
- You may need to prepare a series of questions that will lead you and the delegates to the correct conclusion. Each question can further the delegates' understanding and reinforce their learning at the same time as finding out whether or not the learning objective has been achieved.

- If the answer you get is not absolutely clear, be prepared to rephrase the question.
- Feed back the answer to the delegate by paraphrasing their answer to ensure that you have correctly understood their response and also to reinforce the point.
- Try to avoid adopting an aggressive, interrogational approach to asking questions. Aim to lead a discussion involving all the delegates by the use of questioning rather than concentrating on one or two people. In this way you should be able to assess the group's understanding.

If your questioning uncovers a real flaw in your materials or the session's approach, make sure that you make a note for yourself. You can then rewrite the materials so that you don't make the same mistake in the future. In this way, you can continually improve your training and the results that you get from it.

Setting exercises and action plans

Exercises such as role-play, quizzes, tests and syndicate exercises can not only break up the presentation, providing variety and helping to keep the delegates interested (and awake!), but can also be used by the trainer as opportunities to monitor the delegates' progress. See Chapter 6 for details of how to use role-play and syndicate exercises.

Quizzes and tests, although they require work in advance to devise them, can be the easiest method of evaluating how much of the course has been absorbed by the delegates. You can also set up the test so that it is less formal than an exam (these can cause panic in even the most confident delegate) and can be marked by the delegates themselves and used to generate a discussion of the more difficult issues.

Devising a test

- Ask questions that will show whether or not your learning objectives have been met.
- Try out the test on colleagues if possible.
- Spread out the questions on the page – don't make the questions appear crowded or confusing.
- Use multiple-choice questions – and make the instructions clear.
- Aim for ten questions so that the delegates can easily calculate their scores as percentages.

- Ask a blend of questions – some easy and some more difficult. Start with the easy ones and then progress to the hard ones. Be careful, however, that you take into account the delegates – don't offend them with questions that are just too easy or confuse them with ones that are just too hard.
- Make the order of the questions logical – this will help to reinforce learning.
- Set a time limit – don't make the test too long.
- When the time is up, get the delegates to swap test papers and mark each others' answers.
- Include instructions on your question sheet on calculating their score as a percentage and make sure that you allow space for this.
- Show a range of scores with comments such as 'Excellent' down to 'Could do better'.
- Don't allow this exercise to be taken too seriously in the training room and be aware that a poor performance can be de-motivating. Be ready to point them to the appropriate part of your handouts that they will leave the course with, or offer to help them after the course.
- Ask for the delegates' reactions. If they highlight difficult areas, use their comments to start a discussion and use the opportunity to go back over points that have not been adequately understood.
- Collect the papers after the discussion and take them to analyse later. Look for patterns showing areas where more reinforcement of the topic is necessary.

Action plans

These plans, prepared by each delegate at the end of the training event, are a useful learning tool and provide some feedback for the trainer and for the delegate's manager. They can be a clear pointer as to how the learning will be transferred to the workplace and should be followed up at a later date to evaluate progress and the effectiveness of the training. Having completed the course learning sessions, the trainer should lead the exercise so that an appropriate individual action plan can be prepared by each delegate:

- encourage the delegates to consider the main learning that they have received and the benefits that this could produce related to their work
- get them to say, and record on their individual action plans, how that learning can be applied in their own job

- make sure that they state precisely what they will do and that they set themselves a time limit
- let them know where they can go for help and support when they are back in the workplace
- make sure they are specific – with tasks, improvements and timings

Giving and receiving feedback

Feedback is an essential part of any training session and must always be two-way. You must be prepared to give feedback to your delegates and also to receive it from them. In this way you will be able to improve not only their learning during and after the training sessions but also improve your own performance as a trainer in the future. In your enthusiasm – and all the hard work that training entails – don't lose sight of the fact that training is only useful when the knowledge and skills that are being taught are transferred to the workplace. It is only then that performance can be improved and that is the ultimate goal of training.

With the goal of improving the performance of the delegates at the front of your mind, you should try to make sure that the feedback you give is positive and encouraging. Even if a delegate is obviously struggling with the material, you should try to phrase the feedback so that you mention any positive behaviour you have been able to identify and so that they can see how to improve. Feedback should be used to point the trainees in the right direction and to ensure that when they get back to their jobs they are able to use the knowledge they have gained on your course. If you do not achieve this, then you will not have met your training objectives.

So what is feedback? It is any information that you receive from, or give to, the delegates that can be used to improve their performance or the results of the course, either now or in the future. This information will include:

- answers to questions you ask
- the delegates' body language
- comments made
- results of tests and questionnaires

As feedback must be a two-way affair it will also include:

- all the comments that the trainer makes on the trainees' performance

- all the advice he or she gives
- all the updates on how the learning objectives are being met

It is only when trainees receive feedback that they can alter their behaviour to ensure a better chance of improving their performance and achieving their goals. They need to know whether or not they are achieving goals, that what they are doing in the training exercises is at an acceptable level, and that they are on the right track.

It can be difficult to give positive feedback but a good trainer will develop ways of finding encouraging things to say. It seems to be human nature to find it easier to find faults in people's behaviour and performance but you, as the trainer, must work on finding at least twice as much positive feedback as negative. It is only by doing this that the trainees will be motivated and encouraged and, of course, this is an ideal frame of mind to be in when learning. They will learn far more if the trainer can induce this feeling in them than if he or she takes the easy route and merely finds fault.

Another important element of effective feedback is timing. If at all possible you should give the feedback during the training session as people soon forget exactly what they were doing and how. Bearing in mind that any feedback given in public must be positive (if there is any negative element to the comments, then you must create an opportunity to give the feedback in private) so that the delegate is not embarrassed or discouraged. If delivery of the feedback is delayed then it will be far less effective.

Apart from the type of feedback (positive rather than negative) and the timing of it, how you deliver feedback is also important. It is essential that anything you say about the delegates' performance is specific. Don't be tempted to offer vague impressions of their behaviour or let your own prejudices inform your comments. Gather your information based on what you have actually seen during the session and then phrase your comments so that the positive elements and encouragement are what the delegate will remember and act upon. Your job is not to judge, but to state what has happened as simply and positively as possible and to highlight the results of the actions. This process does require a lot of effort and thought on the part of the trainer and must be done sensitively. Most trainees will be able to spot insincerity so do not offer empty praise. You might, for example, give feedback after a role-play exercise involving dealing with a difficult customer by saying, 'You handled their objection in just the right way by saying you were sorry that they were upset and also by giving them time to say what they wanted to say. How do you think that went?' (specific praise based on what you have observed and asking the trainee to review their own performance), rather than saying vaguely, 'You handled that well'. The other thing to remember is that you should never make comments on someone's personality. If a trainee feels that they are being personally attacked, then they will be left with a feeling of resentment rather than knowing how they can improve their performance.

The example above also illustrates a further way of developing feedback during your training session – that of self-appraisal. Getting the delegates to consider and give their views on their own performance is a very effective way of improving performance. When the delegate has acknowledged the positive and negative points of their own actions, the lessons learned will be far stronger.

So far, we have mainly considered the type of feedback that you, as trainer, will give to your trainees. However, as mentioned earlier, effective feedback must be two-way. Feedback from the delegates in the form of their written answers to your event questionnaire (more of how to use this later in this chapter) or their verbal responses to your comments on their performance should always be asked for. It is essential that they know before the start of the session that their feedback will be expected and that you will act upon it.

It is important that you do not respond in a defensive way to any negative feedback you may receive from delegates. Try to remain objective – if you allow your personal feelings to surface at this stage you are not only presenting a poor example to your trainees but you are also risking losing your authority and putting yourself in an awkward position. It is just as valuable for you to remain objective when receiving feedback as it is for you to be objective when giving it. Here are some tips on how to receive feedback without losing your authority:

- listen to the feedback – this must be your number one priority
- thank the person giving the feedback
- appreciate that the feedback is (hopefully, if the delegates are following your guidelines about giving feedback) meant positively and is not a personal criticism
- be objective – there is nothing to be gained by taking it personally

- give their comments your serious attention and decide whether the change that the feedback suggests is going to improve your future performance
- consider how you might be able to change if you judge it to be necessary
- communicate your conclusions to the person giving the feedback
- remember that your objective in this situation is to improve your performance

Revision test

After any particularly important piece of learning or at the end of a training event, you may want to plan in a short test to revise the issues and to make sure that your objectives have been met. Keep the following in mind when devising a revision test:

- do not be tempted to try to test the delegates on every aspect of the course or topic – keep it short and relevant and do not let the delegates feel that this is a full-scale examination
- try to keep the test to one side of a sheet of paper
- multiple-choice questions can speed up the processes of both answering and marking the test
- when you've collected the papers, make sure you give the delegates the correct answers

An example of part of a simple test for use at the end of a training session on customer service is shown in Figure 2.

Ending the session

You should always plan a closing session into your course and allow time in it to accomplish a satisfactory rounding-off of the course. The main aim of this session will be to restate the course objectives and demonstrate how they have been met, but you will also need to attend to a few housekeeping issues such as:

- thanking the delegates for their attendance and attention
- the issue of certificates and/or test results, if appropriate
- making sure that everyone collects all their belongings and, if applicable, have checked out of their hotel room

Make sure that you also include:

- a brief summary of what they have learned

IMPROVING CUSTOMER SERVICE

REVISION TEST

1 How should you address customers who telephone with a complaint?

a sir ☐

b by name ☐

c do not use a name ☐

2 When should a complaint be dealt with?

a the same day ☐

b as soon as possible ☐

c within a week ☐

3 Which part of the computer system should you use to record the details of a complaint?

a a piece of paper ☐

b the customer's address file ☐

c a new complaint file ☐

4 Who is responsible for answering the complaint?

a the Department Head ☐

b the Complaints Manager ☐

c the person taking the call ☐

5 When should the complaint file be closed?

a after the complaint has been noted ☐

b after the customer has been told how the problem has been resolved ☐

c after the complaint has been followed up and the customer is satisfied ☐

figure 2 revision test

- any outstanding issues that you have accumulated during the course
- advice to the delegates on what will happen next in terms of assessment back in the workplace
- restatement of the event objective – display it one more time
- an assessment of the course – see below
- some last-minute advice as to how to put their learning to good use in their jobs

Always sum up

Never miss an opportunity to reinforce learning. The summing up at the end of each session must be used for this purpose and can also be used as part of the evaluation process. However, you must be careful that you do not open up this concluding part to questions from the delegates as these may introduce a new aspect to the session that you would not be able to deal with adequately at this stage, so make sure that you have asked for – and dealt with – questions from the floor before your conclusion.

Bear in mind that what the delegates hear last is what they are most likely to remember – so make sure that you make good use of the last few minutes.

An event questionnaire and how to use the results

During your closing session you should hand an event questionnaire/course assessment form to each delegate (see example in Figure 3). Explain that the information and comments that they give will be kept confidential. Advise them that it will be used to assess the effectiveness of the training that they have had and to help you to improve things for the future.

Ask them to complete the forms before they leave and make sure that you collect the completed forms from each delegate. It is not a good idea to let them take the form away with them to fill in later and send back to you as many of them will forget your requirements as soon as they are back in their place of work.

Having got the completed forms back you must take action on the results. First check them for any serious concerns – these may be found in the comments sections – and make sure that you note them to take action when you are back at work.

COURSE ASSESSMENT

We hope you have enjoyed your training and we now need your help to review the event. Please complete this form to give us your impression of the training. Your comments will be confidential and will be used to ensure that we can continue to improve.

Thank you for your help.

Please give each area a score from 1 to 10, where 1 is very poor/not at all and 10 represents excellent.

Area	**Score** 1 to 10	**Comments** please give us your comments on your rating
Course content		
Suitability of the venue		
Trainer's presentation		
Course materials		
Did the course meet the learning objective?		
Accommodation (if applicable)		
Your overall opinion		

Which topics in the course would you remove?

....

Are there any topics that you think should be added to the course?

....

Any other comments you wish to make

....
....
....
....

figure 3 course assessment

Next do a bit of analysis on the scores that have been given. For each area add the scores from each delegate together and then divide by the number of delegates. This will give you the average score, out of 10, for that particular section. Then multiply by 10 to express the average score as a percentage. For example, if you have six delegates who record scores of 10, 6, 8, 9, 10 and 8, this would give a total of 51 which, if divided by 6, will give an average score of 8.5. Multiply this by 10 and you can see that an average score of 85 per cent has been given. Now look at how you can use the scores for each of the question areas:

Course content

This is an important section and your target should be at least 80 per cent. Try to analyse the comments to see which areas are lacking. It may be that the delegates feel that there is a lack of depth in the course or that some important subject areas were not covered.

Suitability of the venue

It is unlikely that delegates will make positive comments in this section. This is fine, as the objective regarding the venue is for it to suit the purpose and be comfortable, so the venue should be unobtrusive as far as the course is concerned. Many delegates will make negative comments in this section and you should take notice of these. It may be that the venue is not at fault, merely that the room layout was wrong or there is some other problem that can be easily put right. Take any comments seriously even if you feel that the delegates are complaining about nothing. The suitability of the venue can have an effect on the delegates' learning and thus have an impact on your objectives. Aim for a score of at least 70 per cent.

Trainer's presentation

Here you need a score of at least 75 per cent. You should heed your own training advice – don't take any comments personally! Take any comments as an opportunity to improve your performance. If this is your first event as trainer, then you will find some very useful information here. You may be told that some delegates couldn't always hear you or that you need to engage with the delegates more – or less. Note their comments and give them some thought when you are next planning a training event.

Course materials

You should aim at a score of 80 per cent or more in this section. Any less and you will need to conduct a complete review of your course handouts to see where you can improve them for future events.

Objectives met?

Your target here should be a minimum of 80 per cent. If you get less than this you will need to review and improve the course content – the comments made against this question may help you to see where the course has not met its objectives. This is the most important area and you must make changes where necessary before you run the event again.

Accommodation (if applicable)

Again you will get some moans here but the comments are still important. Poor accommodation can have a negative impact on the delegates and you may need to sort out any problems with the hotel manager or the person in charge of the accommodation so that problems can be resolved before you are able to use the venue in the future. Alternatively, with more serious problems, you may need to find other accommodation.

Overall opinion

Another important score – aim at 80 per cent or more. Whatever scores you achieve for your training event, do not get too complacent or too disheartened. Many trainees will not be objective and some will not make any comments whatever. This is usually a reflection on them rather than on you or your course. Make sure that you use any comments that you do get to ensure continuous improvement.

Summary

- Evaluation during a training session can be used to improve your performance and can help you to meet your objectives.
- Plan in advance the questions that you will ask during the training session so that you can evaluate the ongoing effectiveness of the training.

- Short quizzes or tests will show you where reinforcement of the learning is necessary.
- Action plans should be prepared by each delegate at the end of the event. These will help to ensure that all delegates understand how they can apply what they have learned and that they are committed to doing so.
- Feedback is the information that you receive from, or give to, the delegates. It should be positive and specific and should be viewed objectively.
- Make sure that you round off a training event with a clear summary that reinforces the learning and deals with any outstanding issues and housekeeping matters.
- An event questionnaire will allow you to evaluate your performance and ensure continuous improvement.

Revision test

1. What is the most important use of questions in a training session?
2. How many questions are ideal in a test evaluating delegates' progress?
3. Name one strategy that delegates can use to prepare to transfer learning to the workplace.
4. Give three examples of feedback that a trainer might receive from delegates.
5. When receiving feedback from delegates, what should be the trainer's first priority?
6. What should a trainer always do at the end of a training session?
7. What is the purpose of an event questionnaire?
8. What is the minimum acceptable score for a trainer's presentation in an event questionnaire?
9. When should delegates prepare action plans?
10. Name three things on which a trainer can obtain the opinions of delegates by using an event questionnaire or course assessment form.

evaluation after training

In this chapter you will:
- **discover the importance of evaluating training**
- **learn how to follow up the training with individuals**

The importance of evaluating any training

Knowing whether or not your training event has met its objectives is essential, so evaluation should be an integral part of your training process. You will need to carry out a wide-ranging assessment of the value and results of the training for a number of purposes:

- to convince your training sponsors (the people who are footing the bill) of the value of the training event
- to reassure the trainees that the training has been successful
- to gain information that will help to improve your training in the future
- to bring the trainees' line managers into the process and prove the worth of the training to them

Not only will comprehensive evaluation help to convince your own boss, and the managers of the delegates, of the value of training but it will also help you to refine and improve the training in your organization.

The information that you will aim to get from your training evaluation is:

- the delegates' response to the training
- the changes in the way in which they carry out their work
- the changes in the way they think about how they do their work
- the changes in the practical ability of the delegates' to carry out their work following training
- cost-effectiveness of the training event

Right from the start, when you are building your course materials or choosing the type of training to offer, you should be thinking about how you will obtain the information that will tell you how effective the training has been. (Don't forget, you should also advise all the delegates at the commencement of their training that you will be monitoring the outcomes.) First, ask yourself how you will know if the training has been a success. The answer to this question will probably be split into different time-scales.

There may be a long-term objective of the training – such as an increase in sales over a set period or a decrease in customer complaints – and this will need to be monitored over time. You will need to compare data (regarding sales, customer complaints or whatever) obtained before the training with equivalent data for an agreed period following the end of training.

In the short term you will need to be certain that the delegates have learned what they were intended to learn. To assess this, you may develop a questionnaire for use by the delegates at the end of the course as discussed in the previous chapter (or set up interviews at the course end as this can be more revealing than a standard questionnaire). Remember, though, that, although important, this will only give you one aspect – the delegates' views – of the course evaluation. It will not give you any information as to the effectiveness or 'value for money' aspects of the course as these can only be assessed over the longer term and with a great deal more information to hand.

In the medium term, you will also need to assess whether the knowledge that you have imparted to the delegates is being used effectively back in the workplace. Measuring this may involve a questionnaire not just for the delegates but also for their line managers. In manual skills and activities, this might be relatively easy to measure a short time after the training has taken place, but this will obviously be more difficult with management skills or where you are trying to make company culture changes. A lot depends upon how specific and focused your learning and training objectives were.

To do any of this type of evaluation you must go back to your initial objectives. As we saw in previous chapters, no training should commence without the required outcomes being clearly defined and measurable objectives being set. You will therefore need to obtain historical data so that you will have criteria against which you will be able to compare your results. It is important that you agree a benchmark at this stage so that you will have a figure against which you can compare the change as a result of the training. Depending on the business need that the training is designed to fulfil, this data could include:

- sickness/absentee records
- sales figures – by area, by product and/or by sales representative as appropriate
- statistics and records of complaints
- health and safety records
- manufacturing statistics such as machine output figures

When you are obtaining this data, bear in mind that you will need to obtain similar data some time after the end of the training so advise your sources of this fact and agree time-scales with them. You will then be in a position to produce statistics following the delivery of the training event that will prove whether or not your training has come up with the solution that your organization was seeking. Close co-operation with the managers of the staff receiving training will be necessary (and, in the case of sickness records and so on, also with the Human Resources Department). You could also use this opportunity to get their views and input regarding the subject matter of the proposed training.

Cost-effectiveness

The request to evaluate cost-effectiveness is likely to come from your boss or board of directors. The people paying for the training need to be convinced that they are getting value for money, as training people is expensive and you will need to be able to prove a measurable return. To do this you will have to keep a close watch on the costs of the training and be able to present a report that shows these costs alongside the real – or expected/forecast – benefits of the improved performance of the delegates.

Keep track of the costs for the entire training event. These may include many of the following:

- your salary (or proportion of it that can be attributed to the training project)
- accommodation
- venue costs
- travel and subsistence
- guest speakers' expenses
- catering
- delegates' salaries
- temporary staff to cover for delegates
- production of materials
- handouts and stationery
- training equipment

Although the task of proving that the training has been worthwhile in terms of benefits, such as financial savings, increased profit, improvements to health and safety performance or time savings, is not an easy one, it is nevertheless one worth attempting. Having compiled the data on costs as discussed above, these should then be compared with the benefits of the training event. Quantifying the benefits will be the trickiest part of this as many of the benefits that you will be analysing will not be purely financial. There may be changes involving the culture of the organization, such as a decrease in occasions of sickness absence or fewer accidents. Wherever possible a monetary value should be put on these changes (how much did the former sickness cost, less the percentage decrease, for example). Don't forget that data produced at this point should follow the same format as that produced prior to the course. It is vital to your goal of proving the cost-effectiveness of the training that a direct comparison can be made between the performance of the organization – and of the delegates – after the training, and the benchmarks set in advance of the course. This is the only way that your training sponsors or bosses and also the trainees themselves will be convinced that the training was worthwhile.

The questions that you need to ask to ascertain the benefits obtained as a result of the training include:

- Is work being done faster following the training? This could give savings in the number of people required to carry out the work or in the time taken to do it.
- Have quality standards improved? This could result in a reduction in wasted products, less re-working, or the need for fewer inspections.
- Have customer service standards improved? In the long term this could give reductions in the amount of time spent on complaints or it could give benefits in terms of increased sales or retention of customers. You may be able to include the costs of gaining new customers in the financial benefits gained from training as it is more expensive to gain new customers than to retain existing ones.
- Have staff retention rates risen or absence rates fallen? If so, you should make savings on recruitment costs or temporary cover.
- Are machine output figures rising following training?

Collate the results for the savings and increased profits that you have identified that are attributable to the training and then insert them into the formula for calculating the return on the investment (ROI) in training:

$$\text{ROI} = \frac{(\text{Benefits less costs}) \times 100}{\text{Costs}}$$

In assessing the cost-effectiveness of the training event, a positive answer to this calculation will signify a successful project; a negative answer shows that the event has cost more than the benefit that has been produced; a break-even event will be shown by a zero result to the calculation.

Don't forget that training will almost always have benefits that are not quantifiable – such as better-motivated staff – or altruistic benefits – such as the contribution to the local community.

Following up with individuals

Apart from proving the cost-effectiveness (or otherwise) of a training event, it is important that a check is kept on whether the required changes in the individuals are produced as a result of the training. You need to prove that the positive changes in the behaviour, knowledge, skills and performance of a delegate have been realized as required. This is necessary whatever training has been provided – whether you have just run your own in-house course or have paid for a delegate to attend a high-level management seminar. You must be able to see the desired changes as a result of attending a training event. It is only in this way that you will be able to improve. In the case of an in-house session, you will be able to make the appropriate adjustments to your materials and perhaps also to your delivery method. In the case of an external event, you will be able to decide whether or not to use that training provider in the future and to assess whether or not the training chosen was appropriate.

Post-event questionnaires

The first way in which you can follow up a training event with your delegates is to send them an event questionnaire about six to eight weeks after the event. You will recall that we have already discussed a questionnaire for use at the end of the course, but one used at this stage will give you further information regarding the effectiveness of the training. By the time the delegates have been back in their jobs for six to eight weeks, they will, hopefully, have implemented some changes as a result of the training and this is what a questionnaire at this stage will discover.

How to create an evaluation form

Consider your aims in creating an evaluation form for use after the training event. You need to find out if the training has met its objectives and whether the trainee is now putting the newly acquired knowledge and skills to good use back in the workplace. An example of this type of form is shown in Figure 4.

POST-TRAINING EVALUATION

It has now been some time since you attended the training 'How to improve customer service' and we need to find out your opinions of the event and to find out whether the training has been useful to you. Could you please answer the questions on this form and return to Mr F Bloggs at Head Office by 23 April.

Either delete as appropriate and/or give us your comments whenever possible.

Thank you for your help.

1 Was the objective of the training made clear to you? Yes/No

Comments ....

....

2 Did the training meet its objectives? Yes/No

Comments ....

....

3 What were the two main things that you learned?

1 ....

....

2 ....

....

4 How will you use these two things in your job?

1 ....

....

2 ....

....

5 How will the changes in the way you work as a result of the training improve your performance?

....

....

....

6 Would you recommend the course to others? Yes/No

figure 4 post-training evaluation form

Tips on preparing and using your own form:

- explain the purpose of the form and how to complete it
- ask short, straightforward questions
- ask simple 'yes or no' questions in addition to questions that require more thought – and a longer answer
- make sure that you ask questions about the course objectives
- avoid leading questions
- find out what the delegates have learned
- do not crowd the form – make sure there is plenty of space for comments as you can often learn a lot from these
- set a date for when the completed form should be returned to you
- transfer the answers from each delegate to a master form so that you can analyse their responses as percentages

Questionnaires will undoubtedly be an inexpensive way to obtain feedback on training and can also be used to check with the delegates' line managers that the training has been beneficial.

Observation

The next method of evaluating performance following training that we will look at is that of observation in the workplace. This type of evaluation can be applied to almost any occupation but will probably be used more often in the case of practical skills training. For example, it will be a relatively straightforward proposition to observe a machine operative setting up a new machine on which he has just received training, whereas it will be more difficult to observe a personnel manager carrying out new disciplinary procedures. Even when being used for evaluation of practical skills training, there are drawbacks to the use of observation. The person being observed may feel self-conscious and this may affect their performance of the task. Also, it can be difficult to set comprehensive observation criteria and to ensure that the observation is carried out in an objective way. However, the aims should be to:

- check whether recently trained staff can now carry out the new procedures for which they have been trained
- assess the amount of change that has taken place
- see whether the trainee's behaviour has changed as a result of the training

It will be helpful to prepare a standard form that can be used both before and after the training event to record the observations. This should break the task down into its component parts and pose questions on the correct way to carry out each stage to which the observer can answer 'yes' or 'no' as they check each aspect of the trainee's performance of the task. In this way a direct comparison, using the same criteria each time, can easily be made. Further evaluation, aimed at discovering the way in which people's knowledge has improved following training, can be carried out alongside the observation. Questioning can be carried out verbally while the job is being done and observed or by the use of a written questionnaire.

Written tests

If you have used a written test at the beginning of a training event to check the current level of knowledge, then it will be a relatively simple matter to test the delegates again and compare the before and after scores. This type of test could apply to training where the objective is to increase the knowledge and understanding of the delegates on a specific subject – for example, health and safety procedures, stock control systems, product details or first aid procedures. A written test would be far less effective in checking the effectiveness of training aimed at improving interpersonal skills such as sales, negotiation, customer service or management.

As always, don't forget to mention to delegates at the start of any training that they will be tested in this way. Knowing that they will be assessed will usually make sure that more knowledge is retained.

Interviews

Interviews can give the trainer an enormous amount of information about the value that has been derived from the training. In the same way that questionnaires can give quantitative information about the changes that have taken place but can also give real insights from the comments sections, so interviews can provide a wealth of information from structured questions accompanied by more open, opinion-type questions that get interviewees talking.

The interviews should not be confined to the delegates. Their line managers should also be involved so that you can find out their views on the value of the training that their people have received and whether or not they have perceived a change in the trainees' performance. You will also be able to check what training they are looking for in the future.

Although interviews can produce useful information, don't forget that they can be very time-consuming and you need to be careful that the process of proving cost-effectiveness does not cost too much!

Appraisals

Annual appraisals are a good way to keep track of the effect of your training event on the work of the individual in the longer term. The appraisal process, used correctly and with the full support of the organization's management behind it, is a wide-ranging opportunity to develop staff and to improve the performance of the organization as a whole. Some of the feedback that you must have to improve your training programme will come from appraisals but this will need careful co-ordination with the delegate's manager (or other person carrying out the appraisal) so that questions are asked about the value of the training. Specific feedback should be solicited about which parts of the training are continuing to prove useful in the workplace and this feedback should be filtered back to you as part of the appraisal process. The one essential thing you should do, therefore, regarding appraisals to add their help to your training strategy is to ensure that staff development is put on the agenda. If you can make developmental issues an important part of the appraisal process and get adequate feedback from the appraisals, then you will have 'done your bit' to further the training culture within your organization.

The organization's training strategy can also form part of the appraisal system. Time should be planned into the appraisal for the person being appraised to express their ideas on future training and for a discussion to take place to ensure that the strategy is the right one.

Following up with customers

If the objective of the training event was to improve performance in an area that directly impacts upon customers, then sometimes you will want to consider following up the results of the course with them. This might be by way of an anonymous survey of customer satisfaction or by a random telephone survey of your customers. This type of evaluation must obviously be handled very carefully and only used when you want to hear – and use – the answers that you get! If you are confident that the training has impacted positively on the service that is being given to your customers by the newly trained staff, then ask away. A survey where the majority of answers are positive can serve as a public relations exercise, pointing out not just the efficacy of the training but also the fact that the company is investing in areas that affect customers directly. If, however, you have any doubts about the answers you will receive from your customers, take care. If customer service procedures, for example, have not significantly improved as a result of the training, you could merely highlight your shortcomings in front of your customers by asking questions about them. In this case you may still want to ask but also to use the call as an opportunity to convince the customer that your intention is to improve or you could use a marketing research company who will carry out the research for you anonymously.

As with all evaluation, you should try to ensure that the results of external surveys are compared with a benchmark. This is not possible, of course, if this is the first customer survey that you have carried out so you must phrase your questions for the survey so that customers are made to consider whether or not they have seen any recent improvements in the areas where the training has taken place.

Presenting your results

Usually a manager who has responsibility for assessing training needs and organizing – or delivering – training courses will have to produce a report following the training that will show whether or not the investment has been worthwhile (that is, whether the training worked). Even if you do not have to produce a lengthy document for perusal by the people who have approved the budget for the training, it is always worth including a summary of the outcomes in your files for that particular training event.

Here is a suggested plan for preparing a training evaluation report:

- outline the purpose of the training and state the learning objectives
- summarize the outcomes – the conclusions you have reached and the recommendations that may have come out of your evaluation

- develop the main body of your report with details of the initial request or need for training that was identified, a brief overview of the training event, how the evaluation was carried out and the findings of that evaluation
- conclude your report with your judgement on the effectiveness of the training
- add appendices if appropriate – these could include a list of the learning sessions in your training event, the data you have used in your evaluation and forms and methods used to collect the data along with details of the cost of the course

A report of this kind is often more effective if you follow the 'tell them what you're going to tell them, tell them, tell them what you've told them' approach as you will have done when designing your course, i.e. start by outlining the training's purpose and why you are preparing the report then follow this by describing the training and detailing its costs. The conclusion should reiterate the benefits of the training and restate the cost-effectiveness. Make sure that the report's recipients are left in no doubt as to the worth and effectiveness of the training.

Make sure that the presentation of your results appears professional – a report littered with spelling and grammatical errors or presented in an un-businesslike way will not impress (even if your training event was a roaring success) and this may affect your training budgets in the future.

Summary

- Evaluation following any training event is essential. You need to know whether or not it has met your objectives.
- Evaluation can be carried out using a questionnaire, staff appraisals, interviews (with delegates and with their line managers) or by observation.
- The results of your evaluation should be compared with the benchmark data that you gathered prior to the course.
- Keep track of all the costs associated with any training so that you will be able to calculate the cost-effectiveness of the event.
- Use an evaluation form sent to the delegates six to eight weeks after the training event when they will have started to put into practice what they have learned.
- Prepare a training evaluation report – including the outcomes – before you close your file on the event.

Revision test

1 Name three reasons for evaluation following a training event.
2 With regard to evaluation, what should you advise delegates at the start of their training.
3 How can you monitor long-term objectives of training?
4 Who would be likely to ask you to evaluate the cost-effectiveness of your training event?
5 If an objective of a training event was to improve quality standards, how could you tell if you had been successful?
6 How long after a training event should you send out a questionnaire to the delegates?
7 How can staff appraisals be used to improve the training process?
8 When might a written test not be effective following a training event?
9 When would you use a survey with customers following a training event?
10 With what should you end a training evaluation report?

In this chapter you will:

- get some final advice
- find further resource suggestions

Congratulations! You've made it to the end of the book. By now you should be well on the way towards meeting your training objectives. You now have the tools that will enable you to carry out a training needs analysis and to set those all-important objectives. You also have the information necessary to make your choice from all the training options available to you and to assess its effectiveness. If you have decided to run in-house training events, you also have details of how to design and run a course or seminar. Good luck!

Finally, just a few more tips to keep you on track:

TOP TEN TIPS

1 Don't forget training for yourself. If you are going to design and deliver a course of your own, take the time to bring yourself up to speed.
2 Set objectives – if you don't know what you're aiming at, how will you know when you've succeeded?
3 A Training Needs Analysis is essential. Find out what your organization needs now and what it will need in the future to fulfil its plans. Find out what skills and aptitudes your people have and then address the gap between this and what the company needs.
4 Get to know the training market in your area of business. Research what training providers are out there and what they are offering.

5. Consider what training you can arrange in-house – induction training, short seminars, discussion groups, on-the-job training, coaching, mentoring and focused projects.
6. Assess yourself – could you be a trainer? – and be honest with yourself.
7. Preparation is the key to a good training course. Find out about your audience, the content of the training, the environment and the equipment – and link this to a clear plan of how you're going to meet your objective.
8. Prepare and use top quality visual aids to vary the pace and content of your course.
9. Keep track of all the costs involved in training.
10. Evaluate both during the training and after it so that you can see if you've met your objective.

And remember...

Training is important. Failing to develop your staff leads to a lack of growth in the organization. You should aim at continuous improvement in performance.

Recruiting the right people is important, of course, but it is just as important to train and develop these people to move your organization forwards and to develop managers who can lead the company into the future. If you can develop a culture within your organization where continuous improvement is the aim – and the norm – you will achieve success.

Improved skills lead to improved performance!

Useful reading

Boydell, Tom, *A Guide to the Identification of Training Needs*, (BACIE) 1983

Bramley, Peter, *Evaluation of Training – A Practical Guide*, (BACIE) 1986

Kamp, D., *The Excellent Trainer* (Gower) 1996

Kroehaert, G., *Basic Training for Trainers*, (McGraw-Hill) 1995

Mehrabian, A., *Non-Verbal Communication*, (Aldine Atherton) 1972

Oppenhaiem, A.N., *Questionnaire Design, Interviewing and Attitude Measurement*, (Pinter Publishers) 1992

Peel, Malcolm, *Successful Presentation (in a week)*, (Hodder & Stoughton) 1998

Seifert, L. and Stacey, M., *Troubleshooting for Trainers – Getting it Right when Things Go Wrong*, (Gower) 1998

Useful organizations and websites

www.acompletecv.co.uk
Details of the cenres offering the ECDL (European Computer Driving Licence) qualification are listed here and information on how it can help your business.

www.businesslink.gov.uk
Business Link is a government-funded network of local advice centres for business. The website includes a database of courses and events.

www.chamberonline.co.uk
Local Chambers of Commerce are good sources of information on local training suppliers.

www.elearningnetwork.org
The e-learning network aims to provide a lead in the use of learning technologies.

www.ipd.co.uk
The Institute of Personnel and Development has plenty of information on all areas of training from a human resources viewpoint.

www.learndirect-business.co.uk
Learndirect have a learning advice line and also offer cost-effective online courses.

www.microsoft.co.uk
Find hints and tips on using PowerPoint on Microsoft's site.

www.open.ac.uk
The website of the Open University.

www.tradingstandards.gov.uk
The Trading Standards Department of your local council may supply courses to help you meet their requirements.

www.trainingsupersite.com
A magazine website with articles and resources on training.

www.venuedirectory.com
Venue Directory has details of meeting and event venues worldwide.

Chapter 1

1 Evaluate the business.
2 Communication, staff retention, motivation.
3 A training needs analysis.
4 Staff, suppliers, customers.
5 Interviews, tests, references, log books, work samples.
6 The one that is both urgent and important. It must make a difference now.
7 Ask them.
8 A reduction in the number of complaints or returned goods or an increase in sales.
9 To improve the performance of the business.
10 To avoid losing them to the competition.

Chapter 2

1 Budget, time available, urgency, training objectives, subject.
2 Ask two questions – what does the trainee already know and what is their level of education?
3 Skills courses.
4 Experience, knowledge, networking, motivation.
5 Tutorials for word processing or spreadsheets.
6 Via e-mail or by logging on to a website.
7 Implement a coaching programme.
8 It involves intervention while allowing development within the job. It is not training in new skills but correction of application of skills that already exist.
9 Breakdown of the organization's methods of communication.
10 To identify needs and opportunities.

Chapter 3

1 Mission Statement, a family tree, what the company does, participation and commitment of senior management, useful information, the chance to ask questions.
2 The 'buddy system'.
3 To find out whether or not the trainee has understood the process.
4 It must be two-way.
5 Role-play, planned discussion, brainstorming.
6 When the training task will need to be repeated with various members of staff over a period of time.
7 To resolve cultural issues that can lead to stress-related problems.
8 Mentoring.
9 Sourcing exercises, reports on competition or on a company's efficiency, creative thinking, customer satisfaction surveys.
10 Training, eases a new starter into the organization, prevents problems.

Chapter 4

1 Specific, Measurable, Achievable, Realistic, Timed.
2 Travel, accommodation, course materials, venue costs, trainer's fees.
3 Contribution to the community.
4 Delegates who feel uncomfortable with written materials.
5 Do your research carefully.
6 Budget.
7 Content that applies to many organizations rather than specifically to an individual organization's circumstances and needs.
8 Recommendation, Chambers of Commerce, Business Link, local colleges, Learndirect, local council, the internet and Yellow Pages.
9 Discipline.
10 Use the self-assessment form entitled 'Could you run a training event?'

Chapter 5

1 Age, gender, ethnicity and religion, educational level, current concerns, motivation.

2 Achievement and recognition.
3 Syndicate exercises, interviews, group working, discussions.
4 All tables/desks in rows, facing the front of the room.
5 The same running order and structure as the training session.
6 Manufacturers' instruction booklets, company brochures and newsletters, government and professional bodies' leaflets.
7 At the end of the training session.
8 It is the one most commonly found available in organizations.
9 Include variety and tailor the material to suit the delegates.
10 What do you want the delegates to have learned at the end of the session?

Chapter 6

1 Write it down, keep it in front of you and expand it.
2 To sum up the content and the aim of the training and also to arouse interest.
3 Put topics on cards, note extra ideas, move cards around to get to the right order.
4 The main body.
5 Use a statistic, quotation, anecdote or story.
6 Learning objectives, duration, start and finish times, housekeeping details, materials, equipment, notes on delivery.
7 30–40 minutes.
8 Questions.
9 Specially designed training room, boardroom, spare offices, canteen.
10 Schools and colleges, local authority facilities, village halls, museums, art galleries.

Chapter 7

1 Preparation.
2 Attention focused on the speaker, leaning forward, nodding.
3 Over half.
4 Stand up.

5 No one should interrupt, no one allowed to dominate the discussion, everyone should be prepared to justify and explain their views.
6 If they didn't understand something, then someone else will certainly have the same problem.
7 Display a slide or write the objective on a flipchart.
8 Brief prompts on cards.
9 Syndicate exercises, quizzes, brainstorming sessions, video material and discussions.
10 Arms crossed in front of bodies and hands on faces or over mouths.

Chapter 8

1 Flipchart.
2 Prepare in advance.
3 Take it away, as leaving it displayed can distract the delegates.
4 A flipchart or spare projector.
5 Just one.
6 Laptop, disk, projector, cables, battery, notes.
7 Content, volume settings, quality.
8 After planning the sessions.
9 They enhance your message, break up the presentation, help to avoid boredom and make it easier to understand.
10 During your presentation as it will distract the delegates.

Chapter 9

1 The Analytical Type.
2 Videos.
3 Minimize disruption and remain in control.
4 Encouragement, positive body language, extra explanation of materials.
5 Restlessness, lack of participation, little enthusiasm or commitment, answering perfunctorily.
6 The Innovative Type.
7 Quickly, often acting on hunches.
8 The Passive Type.
9 Handouts with plenty of information, exercises.
10 Don't take it personally, keep learning objectives in sight.

Chapter 10

1 Evaluation.
2 Ten.
3 Action plans.
4 Answers to questions, comments, body language, test results.
5 Listen.
6 Sum up.
7 To assess the effectiveness of the training and to help to improve things for the future.
8 75 per cent.
9 At the end of the training event.
10 Content, venue suitability, trainer's presentation, course materials, accommodation.

Chapter 11

1 To prove the value of the event, to reassure trainees, to gain information to help with future courses and to involve line managers.
2 That you will be monitoring the outcomes.
3 By comparing data obtained before the training with equivalent data following the training.
4 Your boss or board of directors – people paying for the event.
5 A reduction in wasted products, less re-working, need for fewer inspections.
6 6–8 weeks.
7 By ensuring that staff development is put on the agenda, asking questions about the usefulness of training and future requirements at appraisals.
8 For courses aimed at improving interpersonal skills.
9 When you want to hear – and use – the answers and when you are confident that the training has had a positive effect.
10 Your judgement on the effectiveness of the training.

index

accommodation **125**
action plans **116–17**
age of delegates **58**
analytical learning style **104–5**
anxious types **109**
appraisals **6, 9, 136**
aptitudes **19, 57–8**
assessing training needs **4–5, 8–12, 56**
assessment of courses **122–5**
assessment of prior learning (APL) **11**

benchmarks **129**
benefits and costs analysis **45–6, 49, 130–2**
body language **85–7**
boredom **65, 84**
brainstorming **36, 67**
buddy system **31–2**
budgets **19, 48**
  cost effectiveness **45–6, 49, 130–2**
business evaluation **4–5**
Business Link **50**

CD-ROMs **23–4**
Chambers of Commerce **50**
change **4, 7–8, 12**
choosing
  courses **18, 46–7**
  providers **50–1, 53**
closing sessions **69, 120–2**
coaching **27, 34–5**
commitment **5–6, 31**
communication **5–6, 10, 27, 35–7**
computers **7–8, 22–6, 97–8**
content of courses **57, 70–3, 124**
correspondence courses **23**
cost effectiveness **45–6, 49, 130–2**
courses and seminars **18–21**
  assessment forms **122–5**
  choosing a course **18, 46–7**
  correspondence courses **23**
  and culture **47**
  external courses **19, 47, 48–50**
  handouts **61–2**
  in-house courses **48–9, 52, 56**
  management courses **13, 20–1**
  skills courses **20**
  see also delegates; designing a course
creativity **40**
criticisms **72–3**
cross-departmental co-operation **39**
culture **6, 12, 38, 47**

debriefings **6, 73**
delegates
  ages **58**
  anxious types **109**
  body language **84, 85–6**

education levels **58**
ethnicity and religion **58**
gender **58**
greeting **81**
keeping their attention **84–5**
number of **48, 49, 60**
overwhelmed types **109**
problem delegates **107–8**
shyness **109**
standards of behaviour **67–8**
types of **57–9, 108–10**
uninterested types **109–10**
delivery **46, 57, 81–91**
presentation skills **75–6, 82–3**
demonstrations **33**
designing a course **65–79**
body **66–7**
closing sessions **69, 120–2**
content **57, 70–3, 124**
discussion sessions **87–9**
dummy runs **74**
housekeeping matters **68, 74**
introductions **67–9**
length of **46–7, 74**
linking sessions **69**
objectives **65, 67, 81**
planning forms **69–70**
questioning sessions **68, 89–91**
structure **65–70**
time considerations **73–5**
title of event **65–6**
difficult delegates **108–10**
discussion sessions **87–9**
dummy runs **74**
DVDs **23–4, 98–9**

emails **6**
environment for learning **76–8**
see also venues
ethnicity and religion **58**
evaluation after training **44, 113, 128–38**
appraisals **6, 9, 136**
cost effectiveness **45–6, 49, 130–2**
evaluation forms **6, 132–4**
interviews **135–6**
observation **34, 134–5**
questionnaires **129, 132, 134**
reports **137–8**
tests **135**
evaluation during training **113–26**
action plans **116–17**
feedback **117–20**
questioning delegates **113–15**
questionnaires **122–5**
tests and quizzes **115–16, 120**
experience **21–2**
external courses **19, 47, 48–50**
eye contact **81, 85, 90**

facilities *see* venues
family tree **31**
feedback **25, 34, 72, 117–20, 124**
first impressions **81–2**
flipcharts **94–5**
focused projects **28, 39–40**
following up **132–7**
with customers **136–7**
with individuals **132–6**
formal qualifications **20, 21–2**

gender of delegates **58**
goals *see* objectives
greeting delegates **81**
guest speakers **74**

handouts **61–2**
hands-on learning style **106–7**
hecklers **108**
hotel facilities **77**
housekeeping matters **68, 74**

in-house courses **48–9, 52, 56**
facilities **76–7**
individual needs **19**
individual objectives **9**
induction training **26, 31–2**
innovative learning style **104**
interviews **11, 135–6**
introductions **67–9**

job descriptions **9, 13**
job manuals **27–8, 37**

job satisfaction **58–9**

know-it-alls **108**
knowledge **22**

laptop presentations **97–8**
layout of rooms **60–1**
  see also venues
learndirect **25, 50**
learning
  assessment of prior learning **11**
  computer-based **22–6**
  environment **76–8**
  online **24–5**
  self-contained **23–4, 26**
  styles **65, 104–11**
length of courses/sessions **46–7, 74**

management courses **13, 20–1**
manuals **27–8, 37**
meetings **6**
memos **6**
mentoring **28, 38–9**
mission statements **9, 31**
models **99**
motivation **22, 31, 58–9, 110**
multimedia **25**

needs analysis **4–5, 8–12, 56**
networking **22**
newsletters **6**
note keeping **84–5**
notice boards **6**
number of delegates **48, 49, 60**
NVQs (National Vocational Qualifications) **20, 21–2**

objections to training **5**
objectives **14, 19, 43–5, 65, 67, 81**
  benchmarks **129**
  of customer service **43**
  evaluation **125, 128**
  individual **9**
  of management courses **20**
  of on-the-job instruction **32**
  organizational **9–10**
  of skills courses **20**
  SMART objectives **44**
  and styles of learning **107–8**
observation in the workplace **34, 134–5**
on-the-job instruction **27, 32–4**
online learning **24–5**
Open University **21, 23**
organizational chart **31**
organizational needs **19**
organizational targets **9–10**
overhead projectors **95–7**
overwhelmed types **109**

passive learning style **105**
person specifications **9, 13**
personnel records **11**
photographs **99**
planned discussion **36**
planning forms **69–70**
post-event questionnaires **132**
PowerPoint **97–8**
practice sessions **33**
presentation of results **137–8**
presentation skills **75–6, 82–3**
prioritizing **12, 74**
problem delegates **107–8**
projectors **95–7**
promotion prospects **58–9**
providers of training *see* training providers

qualifications **20, 21–2**
questioning delegates **113–15**
questioning sessions **68, 89–91**
questionnaires **10, 11, 122–5, 129, 132, 134**
quizzes **115–16, 120**

reassurance **34**
records **11**
religion and ethnicity **58**
reports **6, 40, 137–8**
results presentation **137–8**
revision tests **120**
risk-taker learning style **105–6**
role-play exercises **36, 70–1, 115**

room layout **60–1**

sample products **99**
self-contained learning **23–4, 26**
seminars *see* courses and seminars
shyness **109**
skills courses **20**
skills gap **8–9**
slides **96–7, 114**
SMART objectives **44**
sourcing exercises **40**
staff appraisals **6, 9, 136**
staff retention **4, 45**
standards of behaviour **67–8**
stress **38**
structure of courses **65–70**
styles of learning **65, 104–11**
  analytical **104–5**
  hands-on **106–7**
  innovative **104**
  and objectives **107–8**
  passive **105**
  risk-taker **105–6**
summing up **122**
support for training strategies **12**
syndicate exercises **71–3, 74, 115**

talkative types **108**
targets *see* objectives
task descriptions **32**
technology **7–8, 22–6, 97–8**
tests **115–16, 120, 135**
time considerations **19, 48, 73–5**
title of training events **65–6**
Trading Standards Departments **51**
training providers
  body language **86–7**
  choosing **50–1, 53**
  feedback from delegates **119–20, 124**
  keeping delegates' attention **84–5**
  knowing your audience **57–9, 82**
  note keeping **84–5**
  preparation **56–7, 82**
  presentation skills **75–6, 82–3**
  running a training event **53**
  taking questions **68, 89–91**
training records **11**
transparencies **95–7**

uninterested types **109–10**
urgency **19**

venues **46, 57, 59–61, 76–8**
  assessment forms **124**
  hotel facilities **77**
  in-house facilities **76–7**
  room layout **60–1**
videos **98–9**
visual aids **57, 94–101**
  DVDs **98–9**
  flipcharts **94–5**
  laptop presentations **97–8**
  models **99**
  overhead projectors **95–7**
  photographs **99**
  PowerPoint **97–8**
  sample products **99**
  slides **96–7, 114**
  transparencies **95–7**
  videos **98–9**
  when to use **99–100**

Yellow Pages **51**